D1548306

Arkansas Butterflies and Moths

ARKANSAS
Butterflies and Moths

Lori A. Spencer

Don R. Simons, Principal Photographer

With a Foreword by Robert Michael Pyle

OZARK SOCIETY FOUNDATION
LITTLE ROCK

Ozark Society Foundation, Little Rock 72203

ISBN-13: 978-0-912456-25-6
ISBN-10: 0-912456-25-6

11 10 09 08 07 06   5 4 3 2 1

All drawings by Lori A. Spencer
Book design by Phoenix International, Inc.
Cover design by Lori A. Spencer and John Coghlan
Printer: Phoenix International, Inc., Fayetteville and Hong Kong
Arkansas map reprinted from *Arkansas and the Land* by permission of Tom Foti

Library of Congress Cataloging-in-Publication Data

Spencer, Lori A., 1970–
 Arkansas butterflies and moths / Lori A. Spencer ; Don R. Simons, principal photogra-
pher ; with a foreword by Robert Michael Pyle.
     p. cm.
 Includes bibliographical references and index.
 ISBN 0-912456-25-6
 1. Lepidoptera—Arkansas—Identification. I. Simons, Don R. II. Title.
 QL551.A65S64 2006
 595.7809767—dc22

                                                                    2006022716

Ozark Society Foundation publishes regional books and guides on nature and
the environment distributed by University of Arkansas Press, McIlroy House, 201
Ozark Avenue, Fayetteville, AR 72701 (800/626-0090; fax 479/575-6044;
www.uapress.com).

Ozark Society Foundation
P. O. Box 2914
Little Rock, AR 72203

This book is dedicated in loving memory to my Great-Aunt Mary and Great-Uncle Wilbur Beeson, who exposed me to the beauty of Arkansas long before I discovered butterflies.

Most children have a bug period. I never outgrew mine.

—*Edward O. Wilson*

The Butterfly's Guide to Life
(for All Living Creatures)

Emerge into the world with confidence.
Accept change with grace.
Recognize a higher power.
Dance with children.
Appreciate the flowers.
Ride the breezes with friends.
Fly as high as you can.
Show your colors.
Gather together when the world gets cold and dark.
Celebrate life every day.

—Joanna Rivera Stark
MotherNatureLive.com

Contents

Foreword

When my wife, Thea, and I came to the Mount Magazine Butterfly Festival a few years ago, I checked off my forty-ninth state: only Mississippi remains. I knew relatively little about the big trapezoid two states southeast of my native Colorado, but I did know that it was geographically diverse, lush, and certain to harbor an intriguing Lepidoptera fauna. So there we were, watching a fresh blue-black female Diana nectaring all over bright orange Butterfly Milkweed—fulfilling a lifetime's desire for me. Then a couple of jack o' lantern males joined her, and another one landed on the sweaty steering wheel of our rental car. This was Arkansas, for sure!

We came to Mount Magazine at the behest of Lori Spencer, interpreter extraordinaire. I knew that this compact powerhouse was a ranger to be reckoned with and a devoted naturalist, and quickly discovered that she was also a formidable lepidopterist—one with both a passion for the animals themselves and an equal ardor for learning and sharing all she could about butterflies and moths with all who would listen.

This remarkable volume is the result of the marriage of Lori Spencer's consuming enthusiasms. Thanks to her, the good people of Arkansas (and their lucky visitors) finally have a way to acquaint themselves with their rich butterfly resource—and even representative members of the great and obscure company of moths. As something of a connoisseur of state and regional butterfly guides, I find much to celebrate in this one. The charming illustrations will handily make the connection between the author's careful descriptions and the living insects. The splendid live photographs almost fly off the page and into your imagination of summer days afield. The nomenclature and state of knowledge are up to date, and the text is clear, pleasantly readable, and thorough.

All this is admirable, but even more notable is that the book attends to the much more diverse moths as well as the butterflies. While treating the entire list of butterflies recorded for the state, the author has also selected examples from most of the families of moths that one is likely to encounter. This is almost unique among state butterfly books, a brave undertaking on Lori Spencer's part that will prove a huge gift to her readers. How few of us, even naturalists, know many of our neighbors among the beautiful night fliers!

Reading *Arkansas Butterflies and Moths*, one feels spring coming on, and the keen itch to slip outdoors in pursuit of blues and sulphurs, skippers and coppers, swallowtails, ladies, and satyrs. Or maybe to venture forth at dusk, watchful for sphinx moths at the Four O'Clocks, then stay up to wonder at silkmoths dodging bats around the lights. This new book is as pretty as a fritillary and as loaded as a Luna Moth with sheer fascination of its topic. Lori Spencer, and the publishers, are to be congratulated on producing an excellent and innovative resource. To the extent that it introduces new people to the enthralling world of these beguiling insects; prods kids away from the terminal and into the out-of-doors; awakens citizens to the need to conserve habitat for butterflies and their plants; and stimulates further study of Arkansas's natural history, it will have succeeded wildly. I know it will bring us back again to this diverse, bewitching state. Next time I hope to see Duke's Skipper and the Creole Pearly-Eye.

—Robert Michael Pyle

Acknowledgments

I want to thank the many people who helped with the various phases of this book. James Adams of Dalton State College, Georgia, assisted with taxonomy of the prominents, geometers, noctuids, tiger moths, and reviewed the moth descriptive text. Dale Schweitzer of Port Norris, New Jersey, assisted with underwing larvae. Richard Brown, of the Mississippi Entomological Museum at Mississippi State University, answered my questions on several microlepidoptera species. John Burns of the Smithsonian Institution, Washington, D. C., was of great help with the correct identity of several duskywings. Julian Donahue of the Natural History Museum of Los Angeles County, California, also answered several questions concerning microlepidoptera. Jeffrey Slotten of Gainesville, Florida, identified unknown sphinx larvae, and David Wagner of the University of Connecticut confirmed the identification of several larvae. Paul Opler of Colorado State University answered many of my questions and supported this endeavor. Craig Rudolph and Charles Ely of the USDA Forest Service in Nacogdoches, Texas, contributed data from the Southwest Arkansas Lepidoptera Study.

Jeffrey Barnes, Curator of the University of Arkansas Arthropod Museum in Fayetteville, provided the loan museum specimens for photography. The Arthropod Museum is located within the Department of Entomology and is the largest insect collection in Arkansas.

Most of the photographs were taken by my husband, Don Simons, Interpreter at Mount Magazine State Park. Most of the Logan County photos were taken within the park. Steven Hunter, Norman Lavers, and Don Steinkraus supplied additional photos and their credits are given in the Photographers section. These photographs made it possible to reveal the full diversity of Arkansas butterflies and moths.

Carl Hunter enthusiastically embraced this project when I pitched it to him in 1997. He wanted to include it as an addition to the field guides he had written, got the Ozark Society Foundation involved, and the rest is history. It was his idea that this field guide be part of his nature series. I can only hope this book serves the people of Arkansas as well as his books have served them. Field excursions with students from the Mariposa Project 1997 and 1998, in cooperation with the Northwest Arkansas Education Service Cooperative, were valuable in collecting data.

Robert Michael Pyle and Don Simons reviewed the manuscript. Ainslie Gilligan of the Ozark Society Foundation was my editor. Robert Michael Pyle provided invaluable advice, support, and graciously volunteered to write the foreword.

My thanks to the many people on the Arkansas Butterfly List-Serve, whose postings helped create the "Hot Spot" section and have added to flight records since I created the list-serve in 2001 with the help of Kim Smith at the University of Arkansas at Fayetteville. Refer to the Resources section for information on the list-serve. Norman and Cheryl Lavers provided most of the material for the Delta and Crowley's Ridge regions, Herschel Raney for Bell Slough, and Mel White for Little Rock. Rose Maschek and Jim Gaston introduced me to the hot spot to be enjoyed at Gaston's White River Resort.

Julie Holland of the Holland Wildflower Farm, Mary Ann King of Pine Ridge Gardens, State Horticulturist Janet Carson, and Gary Tucker of FTN Associates LTD. answered every question I had about plants. Julie Holland allowed us to take photographs on the Holland Wildflower Farm in Elkins.

Paul Shell of the Arkansas State Plant Board provided updated information on the gypsy moth in Arkansas in addition to nursery resources within the state. I must also extend my gratitude to Arkansas State Parks, the Arkansas Natural Heritage Commission, the USDA Forest Service, and Arkansas Nature Conservancy for allowing me to survey their lands.

My wonderful friend Joanna Stark gave permission to use her beautiful poem. Don Simons, my patient husband, my family, and my friends provided unwavering support and perseverance throughout the project. Finally, I would like to express my appreciation to the Ozark Society Foundation for making *Arkansas Butterflies and Moths* a reality.

Introduction

This all started as fifth-grade homework. Our assignment was to bring an insect to class. I managed to find a caterpillar in a vacant lot beside our house in Oskaloosa, Iowa, tossed it into an empty pickle jar and was done. We covered the butterfly life cycle in our class insect unit, so I soon learned the caterpillar had made a chrysalis. I set it out on the porch and waited for six months. I had no idea what it was, but was curious to find out. I practically ignored that jar all winter, but when March arrived, I looked at the jar upon arriving home from school every day. One day, at the end of April, I came home, looked at the jar, and stopped dead in my tracks. The tan chrysalis was empty, and hanging onto it was a black butterfly with tails and yellow spots on its body. I got excited, grabbed the jar, and ran to show my dad in the back-yard. He and I shared a wonderful moment as we looked at the butterfly, then each other, and he witnessed my epiphany. How many kids get an epiphany at eleven years of age? That tiny creature sparked a fire that never went out. I knew what I wanted to do in life.

A look through the paintings in the *Butterflies and Moths* Golden Guide led me to identify my fluttering discovery as a Black Swallowtail. We took lots of photos of me holding the butterfly before I released it. I read everything I could get my hands on at the library. When I was twelve, my parents gave me William Howe's butterfly book, and I worked hard to understand it. Scientists spend as much time reading as they do in the field. With a homemade net, I built a butterfly collection, and reared lots of butterfly and moth caterpillars. Dad even allowed me to grow common milkweed in the flower garden so I wouldn't have to wander far from home.

My passion came with a price. First, my father decided to put my new knowl-edge to use. My job was to pick off and dispatch the "little green worms," or Cabbage White butterfly larvae, that we didn't want on our broccoli and cabbage. I hardly put a dent in the population by doing this. If I missed a caterpillar, it would end up boiled in the dinner pot with the broccoli and float to the top. My family didn't find eating cooked caterpillars very appetizing, so over the years I got very meticulous. Second, scavenging dermestid beetles destroyed part of the collection I worked so hard to create, teaching me to always use mothballs to repel them. Third, I once pursued a Mourning Cloak through a field of poison oak and had to stay in the house for two weeks, but it seemed like the entire summer.

My ultimate goal of becoming an entomologist, a scientist who studies insects, was what I focused on during the seemingly endless years of junior high and high school. I truly believe that being outside, finding the caterpillar, and watching its life cycle was all part of my journey to understanding not only the butterfly, but the importance of habitat.

I credit several teachers for keeping me interested. These people were not only teachers, they were interpreters who made the world of butterflies come alive for me, and kept me focused on my goal. Mr. Schilke, my violin instructor, had a butterfly collection and brought it to my science class during our insect unit, shortly after my epiphany. He may never know of the seeds he planted that day. My fifth grade teacher, Mrs. Herington, noticed my interest in insects that year and used it the next year in sixth grade. She asked me to present a program on butterflies to help teach the unit to her class. My sixth grade teacher, Mr. Harvey, had me present the program to my own class first. Later, in junior high, Mrs. Herington videotaped my program and used it every year. I had no idea at the time what I was doing was interpretation.

Several professional lepidopterists also kept this flame kindled through their field guides. I cut my teeth on Howe's book, but my identification skills and butterfly enjoyment soared with the help of Robert Michael Pyle's *Audubon Society Field Guide to Butterflies of North America*. I became a member of the Lepidopterists' Society and the Xerces Society, and Pyle rapidly became my mentor. Another professional I credit is Paul Opler, whose guides helped me to better understand the fascinating world of Greek and Latin names in addition to butterfly relationships.

I have always loved Arkansas. My great-aunt and great-uncle retired in Diamond City and we spent a week with them most summers. There were a lot of butterflies and wildflowers for me to study, and I liked the land as much as the wildlife. I fell in love with Arkansas long before I discovered butterflies, and always felt like I belonged here. My acceptance to the University of Arkansas with a research assistantship felt like a sign, and my opportunities to work with Lepidoptera feel like a gift. I am pleased I can share this gift with you.

Purpose of This Book

People connect emotionally and intellectually with butterflies, and interest has been growing in Arkansas for the past decade, hence the need for a field guide. It is my goal that nature lovers from beginners to professionals embrace this book as a helpful resource and pure enjoyment. Leo Paulissen of the Arkansas Biota Survey compiled a butterfly list in the 1970s. He knew butterflies well, and his extensive collection was bequeathed to the University of Arkansas Arthropod Museum upon his death. The main public interest has been in butterflies, so all Arkansas butterflies are included in this book; they are only a small part of the story, so a cross section of the Arkansas moth world is also revealed.

Most of the butterflies and moths in this field guide are widespread throughout the eastern United States and part of the western states. A few of the butterflies found in Arkansas occur in small populations isolated from the species' larger normal range. Quite a few butterflies and moths have the word "common" as part of their name, which really means "widespread" rather than an abundance of individuals.

Personal comments have been added to some of the descriptions to better interpret a species. It is difficult to discern what is too much, or too little, information, and to remain consistent in the text. Hopefully, you will fall in love with butterflies and moths, and will take action to ensure their survival in Arkansas.

Initially, the ambition was to include the adult and larva side by side for every species in the state. It just wasn't possible in terms of time and logistics. There are a multitude of field guides that have been printed on moths, butterflies, and their caterpillars, so it felt like the wheel was being reinvented. Except for a slight style difference and the fact of Arkansas distribution, there isn't much to differentiate my descriptions from those in other field guides. This book should be thought of as a companion to other field guides that cover butterflies and moths across the country.

What Are Butterflies and Moths?

Butterflies and moths are animals: animals that are insects. All insects are cold-blooded invertebrates with an exoskeleton, six jointed legs, three body parts (head, thorax, abdomen), and antennae. Butterflies and moths belong to the insect order Lepidoptera ("leps" for short), which means "scale-wing." This refers to the powdery, microscopic scales on both sides of each of the four wings. They develop in four stages called complete metamorphosis.

Butterflies and moths are scientifically classified so that they can be distinguished from all other animals:

Kingdom Animalia
Phylum Arthropoda
Class Insecta
Order Lepidoptera
Superfamily
Family
Tribe
Genus
Species
Subspecies

What Is a Species?

Each butterfly and moth is a species of insect. What, exactly, is a species? Sometimes when I present a program, I refer to species as a "kind" or "type" of butterfly, and that is a very general explanation. Over twenty-five species concepts are currently being used by scientists. For the beginner's sake, let's use Mayr's Biological Species Concept, which defines a species as "groups of interbreeding natural populations that are reproductively isolated from other such groups." It is based on an ancient definition by Italian botanist Andrea Cesalpino (1519–1603), "Like produces like." A biological species produces fertile offspring, or "children." As an example, Pipevine Swallowtails only mate with Pipevine Swallowtails, and only produce Pipevine Swallowtails. The Pipevine Swallowtail and Zebra Swallowtail occur in the same location, but do not mate for one reason or another, so they cannot produce offspring. Thus, they are recognized as two separate species, but they have enough traits in common to be placed in the swallowtail family.

Geography is one of the best natural barriers to interbreeding and population overlapping. Over time, this can result in what was known as a species becoming split into two species based on genetic and biological differences.

The science of naming was created by Linnaeus some 250 years ago, and consists of a binomial, meaning every organism has two names—a genus and a species name based on Latin or Greek, so they are written in italics. The genus is capitalized and the species is lower case. These names are usually descriptive, referring to color, size, behavior, habitat, geographical location, or other features of the organism. The names of people and places are often used. Latin and Greek word roots and combining forms are a complex area of study and take time to fully understand.

Most of the species that inhabit Arkansas are widespread throughout the United States. However, the population in one area may be different from that of another. Such distinct geographical variants are known as subspecies, with almost no gene flow between populations. My favorite explanation of this complex subject was written by Alexander Klots in *The Butterflies of North America,* by William Howe. Subspecies are written as a trinomial. If one distinct subspecies is recognized in a specific location, then the rest of the population must also be a subspecies. To use the example Klots provides in Howe's book, the Viceroy, *Limenitis archippus,* looks the same throughout most of the eastern part of the country, but it is darker in Florida. This darker variation became a subspecies written as *Limenitis archippus floradensis.* The rest of the mainland population of the Viceroy is subspecies *Limenitis archippus archippus.* Since it was named first, the mainland subspecies is called the "nominate" subspecies. The scientific name is written as the original genus and species, and the species name is repeated as the subspecies name. Notice the other subspecies name describes a specific region. In this field guide I use the subspecies names most agreed upon by Lepidoptera authorities for Arkansas's geographic location in the country. Some leps have form and variation names, but since these names have no formal standing, they are not italicized.

Names are chosen with care. There are rules used in naming animals set by the International Code of Zoological Nomenclature, directed by a commission. No two leps have the same scientific name, so they cannot be confused.

Butterflies and moths have perhaps the most beautiful names of all insects as many are based upon characters in Greek and Roman mythology. For example:

Erynnis brizo brizo—*Erynnis* was one of the Greek evening spirits who brought retribution for murder. *Brizo* may be derived from *briza*, Latin for grape skins after they are pressed. There are two subspecies: the first is in the United States (nominate subspecies), and the second occurs in California. Thus the subspecies in Arkansas is *Erynnis brizo brizo*. This is the Sleepy Duskywing.

Papilio polyxenes—*Papilio* is Latin for butterfly, and *polyxenes* is for Polyxena, daughter of Priam, King of Troy in Homer's *Iliad*. This is the Black Swallowtail.

Speyeria diana—*Speyeria* is in honor of Adolph Speyer (1812–1892), a German lepidopterist. Diana is the Roman goddess of light and life, of the moon and hunting. This is the Diana Fritillary.

Antheraea polyphemus—Polyphemus was a Cyclops that captured Odysseus and his crew, soldiers in the Trojan War, on their way home, but Odysseus eventually outwitted the giant and escaped. The Cyclops imprisoned Odysseus and his crew in a cave and ate several of them. Odysseus made a spear out of a pole and gouged out the Cyclops's eye. Blinded, Polyphemus was unable to prevent the escape of the men, who clung to the bellies of the giant's goats, because Polyphemus only felt their furry coats. The moth is named for the large eyespot on each hindwing. This is the Polyphemus Moth.

Hyalophora cecropia—*Cecropia* is derived from the Greek *kekrops,* the lengendary king of Athens. It is an appropriate name for the king of moths in the United States. This is the Cecropia Moth.

Catocala vidua—*Catocala* is derived from *kato,* meaning below or behind, and *kalos,* meaning beautiful, a combination describing beautiful hind or lower wings. *Vidua* is derived from *vidu,* meaning widowed, and is appropriate for the somber black color of the hindwings. This is the Widow Underwing.

Life Cycle

Watching the metamorphosis of a caterpillar into an adult butterfly or moth is an exciting experience. The life cycle consists of four stages: egg, larva (caterpillar), pupa, and adult, called complete metamorphosis. The Monarch life cycle is pictured for reference.

Eggs (A) are laid by females on or near the plants that the caterpillar will eat, called the host plants. Many species are choosy about their host plants. Some species lay eggs one at a time, some in clusters, some on the ground near the host plant. Eggs may take a few days or several weeks to develop, and then the larva hatches. Its first meal is often its eggshell. The caterpillar begins eating the host plant (there are non-plant host exceptions). Some caterpillars switch hosts when leaves become too difficult to digest. Some caterpillars eat slower during times of high humidity.

The exoskeleton of a caterpillar is flexible, but it can only stretch so far. Caterpillars grow quickly and must shed the exoskeleton. The process of shedding the skin is called molting (or ecdysis). Each stage of the caterpillar between molts is called an instar (B). The caterpillar rests for a bit, and lets the new skin harden. A caterpillar may molt several times. A caterpillar's growth rate increases with each molt, and as it gets larger, it can consume more food. The size of the caterpillar's last instar can yield an educated guess on the size of the adult. If the caterpillar ran out of food or had to endure bad weather, it will pupate early and be a small adult. If it had enough food and good weather, it will be a larger adult.

The last time the caterpillar sheds, it becomes the pupa. For all butterflies except the skippers, this is termed the chrysalis(C). Chrysalises are usually attached to a sheltered surface such as the host plant, or an object like a twig or fence post. Many moths are known for their cocoons, silken bags that enclose the hard pupal cases of many moths and some skippers. Some cocoons incorporate leaves, soil, or other materials. Some moths pupate underground or in leaf litter, with no cocoons. When metamorphosis is complete, the pupa splits open, and the adult crawls out.

The adult's wings are crumpled, and the abdomen is full of fluid, so the adult rests for a while and pumps fluid into the wings, allowing them to expand and harden. This time is known as the teneral period. When the wings are dry, the adult is ready to fly (D). Some butterflies complete the entire life cycle in month or less, and the cycle is repeated several times a year. A complete life cycle of a butterfly or moth population is called a brood. Some butterflies and moths have several broods a year, some only one brood, and some take three to four years to complete a brood.

The life span of adult butterflies and moths is usually very short. The adult is the sexually active stage, and breeding is the most important task to accomplish before death. On average, an adult butterfly or moth lives two or three weeks. There are extreme exceptions. The generation of Monarchs that migrates south and the Mourning Cloak are the longest-lived butterflies, living nine or ten months. The giant silkmoths live an average of ten days, but they do not feed as adults like the butterflies do. They live off fat stores obtained as caterpillars.

A

B

C

D

Survival

Butterflies and moths are faced with all kinds of natural threats. These insects are a very important part of the food chain, and predators, parasites, and fungus can attack each stage of the life cycle. Birds, reptiles, amphibians, spiders, and other insects eat protein-rich leps.

Crab spiders (A) blend in with the centers of many flowers and grab adult butterflies as they nectar. Ambush bugs do the same. Parasite attack is common, usually by braconid wasps and tachinid flies. Females lay their eggs inside a fleshy butterfly or moth caterpillar (the host). If it's a wasp parasite, the wasp larvae hatch, eat the caterpillar's fatty tissue and organs, and then pupate in a cocoon that often resembles a cotton swab (B). The wasps' life cycle eventually destroys the caterpillar. When the parasite is a fly, the adult fly usually emerges from the pupa of the butterfly or moth. Gardeners benefit from allowing braconid wasps into their gardens. The sad part is that these parasites often attack the butterflies and moths that aren't pests!

Camouflage

Camouflage is one method by which adults like the Widow Underwing (C) escape predation. This moth is perfectly camouflaged against the tree bark. Most underwing moths have this advantage. Question Marks and other anglewing butterflies also blend in well with bark. Numerous caterpillars blend in with their host plants.

Safety in Numbers

Many male butterflies can be observed mud-puddling at moist areas, imbibing sodium and other minerals (D). Ever try to sneak up on a puddle club? It's difficult to do without creating a stir. When a predator tries to capture an individual, the butterfly is startled and flies away, and then other butterflies are startled. The predator quickly becomes surrounded by a swirling array of butterflies, making it very difficult to pick off an individual, and most butterflies will escape.

Mimicry

Mimicry, best known as the art of looking like and/or acting like another species, is a way several species avoid predators. There are several types of mimicry. Batesian mimicry is a classic: a good-tasting species is protected by resembling a bad-tasting species. Mullerian mimicry is a little different: two or more distasteful species get extra protection from looking similar to each other. If a bird has eaten any one of them, it has learned its lesson, and will likely avoid all of them.

A

B

C

D

A good example of classic Batesian mimicry is the relationship between the Pipevine Swallowtail and its imitators. The Pipevine Swallowtail larva, as you'll read in the swallowtail descriptive text, consumes pipe vines, which are toxic. The Pipevine Swallowtail (A) is a dark butterfly, and the underside coloring is most effective to mimic, with its blue bands and orange spots. The underside of the Spicebush Swallowtail (B) mimics that of the Pipevine Swallowtail. In addition, the Black Swallowtail, dark female Tiger Swallowtail, female Diana Fritillary, and Red-spotted Purple look very similar, which gives these butterflies a measure of protection from predators, even if the differences are obvious to our eyes.

The Monarch (C) and Viceroy (D) were long considered the best example of Batesian mimicry. However, recent studies have shown that Viceroys are distasteful to predators, too. They still get protection from resembling Monarchs, and vice versa, so they are actually examples of Mullerian mimicry.

The art of mimicry also extends to mimicking objects or animal parts. The Buckeye, a butterfly, and the Io and Polyphemus Moths have large eyespots on their wings. These are thought to mimic a vertebrate eye, and fool predators.

Some moths mimic bird droppings to fool predators. The Goatweed Leafwing, Question Mark, Eastern Comma, Gray Comma, and American Snout mimic dead leaves.

Larvae are some of the best masters of mimicry. Caterpillars of the inchworm family (Geometridae) can hold themselves stiff and look just like twigs. The Double-toothed Prominent larva's upper side is the same shape as a toothed elm leaf. Several swallowtail caterpillars begin life resembling bird droppings, and after a few molts, turn green and develop large yellow eyespots with black "pupils." Some sphinx moths replace their rear-end horn with a "button" that resembles an eye.

Show the Colors

Warning coloration is an effective defensive strategy that advertises to the predator that an individual is toxic. Basically, the adult or caterpillar is brightly colored like a stop sign. These species consume noxious chemicals in their food plants as larvae, and concentrations of the same chemicals are found in the adults. If a bird eats the caterpillar or adult, it gets violently sick, and typically regurgitates the insect. The bird learns to avoid anything resembling that caterpillar or adult in the future. One individual may have to die so the rest of the population may survive!

Males and females of some species have visible color differences. Males are usually more brightly colored than females, presumably to protect females from predators while they are laying eggs. This phenomenon is called "sexual dimorphism," and occurs in some skippers, swallowtails, whites and sulphurs, and brushfoots. Otherwise, to sex an adult one must look for a pair of "claspers" on the tip of the abdomen on a male, and the opening of the ovipositor at the tip of the abdomen on a female.

A

B

C

D

Tails

Bird attack is often evident on the wings of moths and butterflies as a triangular-shaped bite out of a hindwing or as a missing tail. Butterflies and moths can fly without their tails, or some other small section of a wing.

Hairstreaks have a great advantage. These butterflies rest with their wings closed, and most have eyespots near the tails. Predators mistake the eyespots and tails as a head and antennae and attack what they see as a vital area. Hairstreaks also sit and rub their wings up and down, ever so slightly, to increase the effect.

Additional Ammunition

The larvae of several swallowtails not only resemble bird droppings, but they have additional weapons in their survival arsenal. Swallowtail larvae have a retractable fleshy organ called the osmeterium. When threatened, the Y-shaped organ juts out from behind the head and emits a foul odor produced by acids, esters, terpenes, or sesquiterpenes. One of the best ways to observe how this organ works is to gently poke the head of a swallowtail larva. The caterpillar will usually jut out the organ just a little, releasing the scent. If needed, the caterpillar will extend the organ fully, and it can be quite long. The Black Swallowtail (A) and Giant Swallowtail (B) provide good examples of the osmeterium in action.

Many brushfoot, giant silkworm, and slug caterpillars are covered with stinging spines. Poison in some species' spines can pack a powerful punch, so be advised. A reaction could be reddening, welling, bumps, irritation, and even a trip to the emergency room. Some reactions only last an hour; some may be evident after a week. It's best not to handle anything that has spines.

In contrast, some species have spines, long filaments, or horns that look dangerous, but they are completely harmless. The Hickory Horned Devil, the caterpillar of the Regal Moth, is one of the largest caterpillars in the country (C), but is rarely encountered. It is named for its ferocious-looking but harmless horns (D).

Overwintering and Migration

Butterflies and moths have adapted to surviving cold winters in a temporary rest, or dormant, period known as diapause. During diapause, movement, growth, and development stop; metabolism, heartbeat, and breathing slow down. Glycerol, also known as antifreeze, is a sugar in the blood of some insects to prevent the fatal formation of ice within the body. Insects can be said to "overwinter," a term used frequently throughout the descriptive text. Each species overwinters in a specific stage of the life cycle. Some spend the winter as an egg, some as immature or nearly full-grown larvae. For many, winter is spent as a pupa. Some species spend the winter as adults, sleeping under bark, in log piles, in leaf litter, or even between two cement blocks.

A

B

C

D

They can be seen flying on warm winter days, so it is not true hibernation. Some adult species cannot overwinter this way and have to move south, then return north in the spring, a two-way movement termed migration. Monarchs are the most famous for their migration, although Buckeyes, Painted Ladies, and some other butterflies undergo this kind of movement. See the Monarch descriptive text on page 106 for more information on migration.

Behavior

Butterflies and many moths are not only a source of beauty, but watching them is a tremendous source of enjoyment. Who hasn't envied, just a little bit, just their ability to fly? Feeding, basking, mud-puddling, courtship, mating, and other behaviors are fascinating to watch and help us understand each species better.

For each butterfly-watching excursion, you should first have a copy of this guide. Binoculars, a notebook and pencil, and a camera are helpful. Many people thrive on the challenge of photographing skittish butterflies, and carefully spread a moth's wings without scaring it away. Sometimes butterflies are so absorbed in their activities, it seems they ignore humans creeping up on them for a closer look.

One of the easiest ways to watch behavior and add to your own personal butterfly and moth checklist is to visit a variety of habitats during different seasons. Habitat is wonderfully variable in Arkansas, including forests, cedar glades, savannahs, swamps, prairies, watercourses, and gardens.

Frankly, I have had some of the most fun watching butterflies on animal scat, especially coyote and bear! Baiting a tree trunk with a sugar mixture yields some interesting animal results, too. Arkansas is one of the few states where you can bait at tree for moths and find black bear claw marks and scat the following day. Bears have been known to rip apart entomologists' tent traps used for research. If you are going to study butterflies and moths in Arkansas, you should be "bear aware." You will find information on bear country safety on websites for most agencies in the Resources section. Chances are better, though, that you will see your "lifer" butterfly than a black bear.

Nectaring and Mud-Puddling

The easiest habitats to access are open gardens or meadows filled with flowers. Butterflies and some moths drink the sugary liquid (nectar) from flowers with their strawlike proboscis, a behavior called "nectaring." Flower nectar is different from flower to flower, and is discussed more thoroughly in the Butterfly and Moth Gardening section. Adults are full grown, so feeding is for energy and egg production, not growth. Flower nectar is not the sole adult resource for many butterflies. Some male butterfly species gather at damp places to drink mineral salts, a behavior called "mud-puddling." Males not only need these salts for themselves, they pass them to the female during mating, which helps her produce eggs. Males and females are sometimes found drinking from carnivore scat, horse urine, and rotting animal carcasses. Nothing in nature is wasted.

Courtship and Mating

Courting and mating are important parts of butterfly and moth behavior. Male butterflies and moths seek females, either by patrolling, perching, or hilltopping. Males patrolling for females fly in areas where females are likely to be. Perching males sit and wait until a female appears flying down a path or some other opening. Since butterflies and moths don't see great detail at a distance, they typically fly up and investigate anything that moves. Hilltopping refers to males flying to the top of a hill where they can get the best view of females working their way up.

Butterflies rely mostly on vision to find mates. Moths rely more on scent to locate and attract mates. This is why male moth antennae are more elaborate, clearly visible on Polyphemus, Luna, and Cecropia Moths. See the Giant Silkworm and Royal Moths description on page 185 for additional information.

Once a female is located, courtship begins. The male either flies above or behind the female, with a fluttering motion. If the female is receptive, she'll land nearby. Mating may take a few minutes to a few hours. The male uses claspers on the tip of his abdomen to clasp the tip of the female abdomen. They may fly while connected, one sex carrying the other.

A mated female usually avoids the advances of males. When she is not receptive, she flips her abdomen up in the air so the male can't get close. Several sulphur butterfly species adopt a different strategy. If a male tries to approach, the female takes a spiral flight into the air, and keeps on going until the male stops.

Basking

As cold-blooded creatures, butterflies and moths need warm flight muscles (as warm as 85–100 degrees), but the air does not have to be this warm. Butterflies orient their wings to the sun, an activity known as basking. Most butterflies bask with their wings open to the sun, which is called dorsal basking, but whites and sulphurs bask with their wings closed, tilted at a 90-degree angle, called lateral basking. Butterflies bask long enough to fly well. If a cloud moves over the sun and causes just a slight change in temperature, butterflies will land until they can warm back up. Darker butterflies warm up quicker, and fly earlier in the day. Much like humans, butterflies don't function well in extreme heat, so they roost on a shady leaf or tree limb during the hottest parts of the summer day and fly in the early evening before the sun sets.

Most moths fly at night and do not use the sun to warm their flight muscles.

Moths have thicker scales than butterflies, which is responsible for their furry appearance. Moths produce heat internally by vibrating their muscles, called shivering, and their heavy scales insulate them.

Butterfly and Moth Importance and Conservation

The order Lepidoptera is in a third place tie with Diptera (flies) for sheer number of species. There are approximately 265,000 species of butterflies and moths on the planet. About 20,000 are butterflies. Most butterflies and some moths are important plant pollinators, second only to bees. They are also a good source of food for other animals. A few butterfly and moth caterpillars are pests, and do a considerable amount of damage to farms, gardens, and clothing. The most notable among these in Arkansas are the Cabbage White, Pink Bollworm, Corn Earworm, Tobacco Budworm, armyworms, and cutworms. It is important to remember that there are fewer pests than beneficial species.

The citizens of Arkansas have a rich butterfly and moth heritage to enjoy and conserve. Still, the areas butterflies and moths inhabit are constantly changing. The butterfly and moth population has changed since early papers were published by collectors in the late 1960s and 1970s. I remember tagging one hundred Monarchs and admiring Great Purple Hairstreaks in a vacant lot covered with asters in 1996 in Fayetteville that is now an apartment complex. As urban growth continues, habitat disappears. Without habitat, we have no butterflies and moths. Butterflies and moths are sensitive to environmental changes and are biological indicators that determine the overall health of an ecosystem. In addition to development, herbicide use, pesticide use, and too little or too much rainfall have led to the loss of habitat.

On the bright side, butterflies and moths have recently been found in places they never were before, mostly due to public awareness and subsequent conservation efforts such as effective management regimes like the highway wildflower program, mowing, prescribed burning, thinning, and natural pest control practices. Gardening has always been popular in Arkansas, and people are increasingly interested in enhancing their gardens to attract butterflies, moths, birds, praying mantids, ladybugs, and other wildlife. Gardening is a form of land management because it provides habitat for all kinds of wildlife. Butterflies such as the Brazilian Skipper have recently formed at least temporary colonies in gardens with cannas. Of course, more people are looking to enjoy a glimpse of these creatures, too. That can only be good news for these creatures' survival.

State parks, national forests, national wildlife refuges, Game & Fish wildlife management areas, and even private landholdings protect habitat of several species not easily found elsewhere. The Arkansas Natural Heritage Commission and The Nature Conservancy have acquired natural areas that provide habitat, and it is unlawful to collect on these sites.

The Arkansas Natural Heritage Commission (ANHC) maintains as one of its responsibilities the keeping of records of rare insects in the state, as does the USDA Forest Service within the national forests. This data has bearing on preservation programs and management regimes. Several butterfly and moth species are considered imperiled or vulnerable and are tracked by these agencies. The contact information for these agencies is listed in the Resources section.

Thoughts on Collecting

Most people prefer to enjoy butterflies by simply watching, rearing and releasing, or photographing them. "Collecting" has become a dirty word of late, and that is unfortunate. As mentioned before, I made a collection when I was younger, and now I make educational collections with the proper permission. I've presented programs for years using a "catch and release" method without harm to any butterflies. To understand and appreciate the butterflies and moths, we must be exposed to them in order to make not only an intuitive connection, but an emotional one that inspires us to act. Encountering them, holding them, being in their habitat, and even viewing them in a collection, are the ways we inspire stewardship in our citizens.

Although I celebrate people's passion for conservation, collectors should not be viewed as the bad guys. Butterflies and moths are great reproducers with short life spans, and more impact is certainly done by vehicle grills than by decades of collecting.

There is a danger of undercollecting. New species are discovered all the time, some from Arkansas, and specimens must be collected as vouchers for scientific documentation. Comparative studies are made with DNA, and for many species, genitalia must be dissected before an accurate identification can be made.

If you are going to collect, do it responsibly and correctly with the proper equipment, labeling techniques, and knowledge of which butterflies and moths are considered vulnerable in Arkansas. Such knowledge can be gained from this guide, personal contact with me, the ANHC, or the USDA Forest Service. Collecting, mounting, and rearing details are not included in this guide. I have included Dave Winter's basic techniques manual in the Resources section, and recommend visiting the Lepidopterists' Society website listed in the Resources section to read their collecting policy.

Always remember that a mounted specimen without a label is worthless. It's history! Specimens carefully prepared and maintained can last for years and reveal important trends such as localities of decline. One third of the photographs in this book are of mounted specimens, which were included to provide a wider representation of our Lepidoptera heritage. I would not have been able to do this without collectors. If a collection is well cared for, vouchers will last for years. An example is the upperside photo of the Brazilian Skipper used in this guide. The specimen was collected in 1911!

Caterpillar and Adult Anatomy

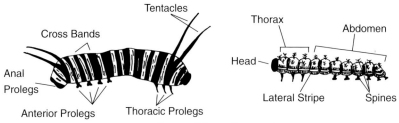

Caterpillars (Larvae)

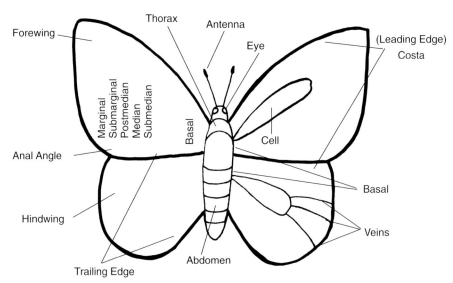

Adult Upperside (Dorsal)

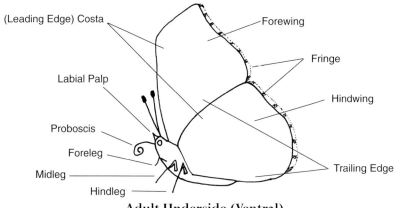

Adult Underside (Ventral)

How to Use This Book

Example: you see a large insect with four black wings and two tails in the middle of the day, and you suspect it is a swallowtail, but are not sure. Is it a butterfly, or is it a moth? Look at the antennae extending from the top of the head above the eyes, body size and shape, "hairiness," and behavior, and match it to the drawings and descriptions in this table:

Butterfly or Moth?

BUTTERFLIES	MOTHS
Clubbed or hooklike antennae	Threadlike, comblike, or feathery antennae
Slender bodies, not very hairy	Thick bodies, usually hairy
Fly during the day	Fly day or night
Wings closed at rest	Wings open at rest

You have determined the insect is a butterfly, and now you want to identify it to family. Look at the size and shape of the wings; you have already noticed the tails on the hindwings and the clubbed antennae. Use the Butterfly Families Silhouette Key that follows to get to the proper family. For this example, the butterfly silhouette matches the swallowtails, so find the page number in the Table of Contents where the swallowtail family begins. Look through the photos, read the descriptions, look at the state distribution, and find the best match to the black swallowtail you found.

If you found a moth instead, try to match it to the silhouettes in the Common Moth Families Silhouette Key that follows next. Due to the large number and diversity of moth shapes, only the large common families are illustrated. Remember, too, that only a cross section of moths is treated in this book. You'll have to flip through the photographs and read the descriptions. If need be, consult additional references. This process is also necessary for the occasional stray butterfly you might see.

Butterfly Families Silhouette Key

Does the butterfly have clubbed antennae? If yes, keep going. If no, go to the bottom.

Is the butterfly large? Tails or no tails?

Tails: Swallowtails (Family Papilionidae)   No tails: Brushfoots (Family Nymphalidae)

Is the butterfly medium-sized?

White or yellow: Whites and Sulphurs
(Family Pieridae)

Dark colored with angled wings:
Brushfoots (Family Nymphalidae)

Is the butterfly small to medium-sized? Tails? Is it white, yellow, blue, copper, metallic, checkered, or does it have eyespots?

Tails: Hairstreaks,
Eastern Tailed-Blue
(Family Lycaenidae)

Coppers and Blues:
(Family Lycaenidae)
Whites and Sulphurs
(Family Pieridae)

Metalmarks (Family
Riodinidae)

Eyespots or check-
ered: Brushfoots
(Family
Nymphalidae)

Does the butterfly have hooked antennae?

Skippers

Common Moth Families Silhouette Key

Is the moth medium to large? If yes, keep going. If no, go to the bottom.

Does the moth have feathery antennae?

Wings drooped at rest: Giant Silkworm Moths (Family Saturniidae)

Does the moth have threadlike antennae?

Long, large forewings: Sphinx Moths
(Family Sphingidae)

Rounded or pointed wings: Underwings and
other Noctuids (Family Noctuidae)

Is the moth small to medium-sized? Wings spread out or pointed down?

Wings spread out flat:

Inchworms, Spanworms, and Loopers
(Family Geometridae)

Wings spread in a "T:"

Plume Moths:
(Family Pterophoridae)

Wings pointed down like an arrowhead:

Pyralid Moths:
(Family Pyralidae)

Prominents:
(Family
Notodontidae)

Fruit and Leafroller
Moths: (Family
Tortricidae)

Tiger Moths:
(Family Arctiidae)

Interpretation of the Descriptive Text

Today there are many different butterfly and moth field guides to choose from, and each author and organization has an opinion on what species concept, species order, and common names to use. The butterflies are the most familiar to the public, and in this book required the most descriptive and interpretive text. Most people are familiar with names like Monarch and sulphur without even knowing what these butterflies look like. Taxonomists study species relationships that help us understand order and stability. The subsequent scientific order of names, called phylogenetic order, begins with what is considered the most primitive species and moves toward the most advanced. However, in this book, that would have entailed writing the descriptive text for the microlepidoptera first, then skippers, true butterflies, and then going back to moths. My goal is to reveal, not confuse, and that is why separate butterfly and moth sections are provided.

The butterfly and moth sections are arranged by family. To review, a family is a grouping of species that share several common traits. In recent years, butterfly families have been lumped together, split, and lumped together again. Taxonomic authorities do this to reveal relationships between species, not to confuse people.

All Arkansas butterfly species are covered in the descriptive text. With a few exceptions the butterflies follow the order of Paul Opler and Andrew Warren's *Butterflies of North America. 2. Scientific Names List,* and common names are given according to Opler's *A Field Guide to Eastern Butterflies.* There are several skippers without photos. To place them in their proper order would have caused printing difficulties, so they are described at the end of the skipper section, pp. 58–60 before the strays. Elsewhere, the butterflies without photos are interspersed into text as close to their phylogenetic order as possible, usually following the description of a butterfly within the same genus. See, for example, pp. 90–94. The Arkansas Butterfly Checklist lists the species in order, including the strays.

The strays, which are species that occasionally wander into the state, are listed at the end of each family, as are species believed to have been extirpated, and those considered to be infrequent colonists as they have not been observed in over thirty years.

An estimated 2,500 species of moths occur in Arkansas. Let's face it, moths don't get much attention. Why? Most people think they are rather drab, when really many moths are spectacular. Many moths fly at night, and not many people are actively searching for them. However, life doesn't stop once the sun sets! There isn't enough time or space to cover them all in a field guide. Therefore a cross section of families, approximately 1 in 20 species, is covered in this book. Species and families were chosen for a variety of reasons. The goal is to familiarize the reader with the characteristics of the large or more common families. Some, however, were chosen for their popularity and familiarity, like the giant silkworm and sphinx moths. Some were chosen because they are crop and garden pests. The moth families not pictured are described at the end of the moth descriptive text. With a few exceptions the moths pictured follow the order of the *Check List of the Lepidoptera of America North of*

Mexico, by Hodges et al., and common names are given according to Charles Covell's *A Field Guide to the Moths of Eastern North America.* A few scientific names have changed since these two books were published, and these updates are reflected in the text.

Each butterfly and moth species description in this field guide contains the following information:

The common name is listed first, then the scientific name on the far right, except for instances in which a moth does not have a common name. If the butterfly or moth has a second familiar common name, it is listed as "aka" (also known as). For each adult, the upperside or underside pictured is listed for the photo, as is the sex when species identification may be made based on sexually dimorphic coloration. Universal symbols for males and females are used: ♂ for male, ♀ for female. For each photo, the county where the species was photographed and/or collected is listed to create county vouchers. Refer to the Arkansas map on p. 24 for counties.

Wingspan is the measurement from left wingtip to right wingtip made from collected specimens and given in inches for convenience. This is meant to be a guide, not an absolute figure. The relative size of adult butterflies and moths is determined by variables such as season, climate, weather, and host plant availability. For several species one sex is larger than the other. Because of these different variables, some individual butterflies or moths found in the field or reared in artificial environments may be larger than the measurement given.

Wing color, shape, and other field marks necessary for identification are described for each species. Descriptions are general. Refer to the drawings and labels on caterpillar and adult anatomy, to the silhouette keys, and to the glossary for unfamiliar terms.

The breeding status of each species is listed as a breeding resident, summer resident, or colonist and also as number of broods produced each year. This is affected by weather variables, as well as availability and suitability of host plants. Residents breed every year in the state, but a colonist may breed one year and not the next, sometimes for inexplicable reasons.

Flight is listed as the months of the year each species is typically on the wing. Because of our mild winters and unpredictable spring weather, adults often fly on warm days in winter, emerge from chrysalises earlier, or migrate north sooner.

The relative abundance of each species or the likelihood of it within the flight period listed is given at the end of each butterfly's or moth's description. This fluctuates for nearly every species from year to year.

Common—more than 5 individuals seen in an area each year

Uncommon—3–5 individuals seen in an area each year

Rare—no more than 1–2 individuals, and not every year

Local—not widespread within range listed, even with suitable habitat

Each species is listed as being found statewide unless the species is known from a specific Arkansas region or grouping of regions: look at the Arkansas map and region summaries below. Even with the combined efforts of my research, university collections, the Arkansas Butterfly List-Serve, USGS maps, state and federal agency lists, private collections, and private county maps, there is always something new to discover and learn. To me, this book will never actually be "finished," as these creatures are dynamic. I encourage people to "get out there" and enjoy our Lepidoptera resource.

Arkansas Map by Regions

Arkansas is divided into six regions: the Ozark Mountains, the Arkansas River Valley, the Ouachita Mountains, the Coastal Plain, the Mississippi Alluvial Plain, commonly known as the Delta, and Crowley's Ridge. There are two groupings of these regions, called the "Interior Highlands," which includes the Ozarks, Arkansas River Valley, and Ouachita Mountains; and the "Gulf Coastal Plain," which includes the Delta, Crowley's Ridge, and Coastal Plain.

For the purposes of this book the features of each region are summarized. A good source for more information is *Arkansas and the Land,* by Tom Foti and Gerald Hanson; consult also state agency websites (see Resources section).

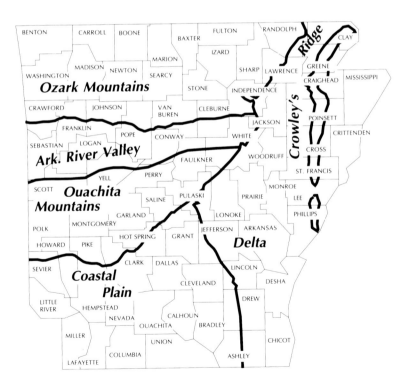

Ozark Mountains

The Ozarks have elevations of 250 to 2,400 feet above sea level. Parts of the region are rugged, with deep valleys, sharp cliffs, bluffs, and ledges. The principal rock formations are sandstone, shale, and limestone. The Ozarks are perhaps the most popularly familiar region of Arkansas, providing the most opportunities for recreation and tourism.

Arkansas River Valley

Between the Ozarks and the Ouachita Mountains there is a different kind of region, the Arkansas River Valley. It is up to forty miles wide. Magazine, Nebo, and Petit Jean Mountains stand high above their surroundings; these mountains have steep sides and flat tops. The Arkansas River flows through the western part of the valley, and there is productive cropland in the bottomlands.

Ouachita Mountains

Unlike the Ozarks, these beds of rock were warped, twisted, and folded. The rock is usually sandstone or shale. The geology of the Ouachita Mountains has had a great effect on the forests of the region as sandstone weathers into a sandy soil that favors pine trees.

Coastal Plain

The lowlands of the Coastal Plain cover most of southwestern Arkansas. This area was once the coast of the Gulf of Mexico. Level and rolling lands, hilly sections, bottoms, and occasional prairies are found here. The sandy hills are good for pine trees.

Delta

The Delta is a land of rivers and wetlands. It covers the eastern third of Arkansas. It, too, was once covered by sand and gravel from the Gulf of Mexico. However, large rivers removed the ocean-bottom deposits. The rivers that shaped the Delta are the Mississippi, the Arkansas, and the White. The result is flat bottomlands, and the areas flooded by rivers are known as floodplains. This area is home to vast farms, and adjacent river corridors providing habitat for abundant wildlife.

Crowley's Ridge

This is the smallest of the regions, and different from all the others. It is in the eastern part of the state, and completely surrounded by the Delta. It "towers" 200 feet above the Delta, and is visible for miles. The rivers left this ridge, 150 miles long and five miles wide, while removing all the ocean deposits from the Delta. The ridge was completed when dust piled up to 50 feet deep. This supports an upland hardwood forest.

Butterfly Descriptive
Text and Photographs

In the end, we will conserve only what we love,
we will love only what we understand,
and we will understand
only that which we are taught.

—*Baba Dioum*

Skippers (Family Hesperiidae)

The skippers are a large family of small to medium butterflies, and are challenging to identify, even for the experts. The skippers are named for their erratic, "skipping" flight, and sometimes they fly by like an orange blur before you can even try to get a good look. Skippers also have "hooked" antennae, which is a way of saying that their antennal clubs are bent, resembling a fish hook.

Three types of skippers inhabit Arkansas: the spread-winged skippers, the closed-winged (aka grass) skippers, and one giant-skipper (Yucca Giant-Skipper). Noticing adult posture may help as you flip through the photographs. Allow for variation in skippers, and several species are sexually dimorphic. Many male closed-winged skippers have a group of black specialized scent scales on the forewings called a stigma that releases pheromones to attract females.

Finding skipper larvae is challenging because they hide during the day and feed at night. Larva identification is even more challenging and most larvae must be reared to adulthood in order to correctly identify them. Many skipper larvae are green or greenish yellow, long, and smooth. Their heads are usually dark and large with a small collar. All our skippers overwinter as partially or fully grown larvae, and pupation takes place either in late winter or spring within a loose cocoon.

There are other field guides that do the skippers more justice than I am able to do within the confines of this book. If you are a skipper caterpillar enthusiast, consider purchasing *Caterpillars of Eastern North America* by David Wagner and *Caterpillars in the Field and Garden* by Thomas Allen, Jim Brock, and Jeffrey Glassberg.

Brazilian Skipper (underside)

A   Silver-spotted Skipper   *Epargyreus clarus*

1) Underside, Logan County
2) Larva, Logan County

Wingspan up to 2½ inches. Unmistakable large silvery spot on underside of
hindwings, gold spots on forewings. Habitat forest edges, gardens, and other
open areas. Breeding resident with several broods. Flight April–December. One
of our most common butterflies statewide.

Larva yellow green with faint cross bands, head reddish brown with two orange
spots. Larvae make tent shelters in host plants of Black Locust, wisteria, and
other legumes.

B   Long-tailed Skipper   *Urbanus proteus*

Upperside, Craighead County

Wingspan up to 2¼ inches. This is the only tailed skipper in Arkansas, often with a
blue-green sheen. Habitat open areas. Breeding resident. Flight July–September.
Rare to uncommon, this butterfly is sighted most often in the Delta and Crowley's
Ridge natural divisions, sometimes in the Arkansas River Valley.

Larva yellow-green, yellow lateral stripes, thin black stripe on top, orange patch
on rear. Reddish head with two orange spots separated by black. Host plants
beans (aka Bean Leaf Roller), Butterfly Pea, Beggar's Ticks, and other legumes.

C   Gold-banded Skipper   *Autochton cellus*

Upperside, Washington County

Wingspan up to 2 inches. Upperside forewings have a large gold cross band, and
a white patch near the tips. Wings have a checkered fringe. The butterfly usually
perches with wings partially open. Habitat riparian areas such as streams.
Breeding resident with two broods. Flight June–September. Local, rare to
uncommon statewide except southern Delta.

Larva greenish yellow covered with tiny yellow dots and two yellow lateral
stripes, red collar, and reddish-brown head with two orange spots. Host plants
Butterfly Pea, hog peanut, beans, and other legumes.

A 1

A 2

B

C

A   Hoary Edge   *Achalarus lyciades*

Underside, Logan County

Wingspan up to 1⅞ inches. Upperside brown, checkered fringe, yellow patch on
forewing. Underside hindwing has large silver-white patch along outer margin.
Habitat open forests. Breeding resident with several broods. Flight April–October.
Uncommon to common statewide.

Larva green to pink with orange lateral stripes, covered with tiny white dots and
hairs, black head. Host plants Beggar's Ticks, wild indigo, and *Lespedeza.*

B   Northern Cloudywing   *Thorybes pylades*

Upperside, Greene County

Wingspan up to 1⅞ inches. Upperside brown, checkered fringe, forewing has
tiny white transparent spots. Underside mottled brown. Face dark. Habitat forest edges and other open areas. Breeding resident with several broods. Flight
April–September. Common statewide.

Larva green to brown, yellow lateral stripes, with tiny yellow spots, black head.
Host plants legumes including *Lespedeza* and Beggar's Ticks.

C   Southern Cloudywing   *Thorybes bathyllus*

Upperside, Logan County

Wingspan up to 1⅞ inches. Upperside dark brown with checkered tan fringe,
forewing with transparent white spot band. Underside brown with dark bands.
Face light. Habitat forest edges. Breeding resident with several broods. Flight
May–September. Uncommon statewide.

Larva and host plants similar to Northern Cloudywing.

D   Confused Cloudywing   *Thorybes confusis*

Upperside, Craighead County

Wingspan up to 1⅞ inches. Aptly named. Upperside brown with checkered
white or tan fringe, forewing with variable transparent white spot-band pattern,
spots near apex slightly curved outward. Face color varies. Habitat river-valley
woods. Breeding resident with several broods. Flight May–September. Local,
rare statewide.

Larva and host plants similar to Northern Cloudywing.

A

B

C

D

A   Hayhurst's Scallopwing   *Staphylus hayhurstii*
Upperside ♀, Crittenden County

Wingspan up to 1¼ inches. Hindwing margins scalloped, checkered black and tan fringe. Upperside ♂ black, ♀ mottled brown with gold flecks. Forewings have dark bands and a few small white dots. Habitat open areas such as forest edges. Breeding resident with several broods. Flight June–September. Local, uncommon statewide.

Larva green with white hairs, head dark. Full grown larvae turn yellow. Host plant lamb's quarters.

The **duskywings,** genus *Erynnis*, are a group of very similar, mostly dark-colored skippers. Seven species occur in Arkansas. Adults usually alight with wings spread, but occasionally you see the underside. They are often encountered puddling and nectaring on flowers. Larvae develop slowly. Full-grown larvae overwinter in leaf shelters, falling to the ground and pupating in a new shelter in late winter or spring. Separating them can be difficult, even for experts.

B   Sleepy Duskywing (center)   *Erynnis brizo brizo*
Dreamy Duskywing (right)   *Erynnis icelus*
Upperside, Logan County

Wingspan of **Sleepy Duskywing** up to 1¼ inches. Long, pointed forewing. Upperside forewing gray with distinct dark gray chainlike bands. Hindwing brown with pale spots. Habitat forest edges, gardens, and other open areas. Breeding resident with one brood. Flight March–June. Common statewide.

Larva green or bluish green with lateral white stripe and covered with tiny white dots. Head brown with yellow-orange patches. Host plants members of the oak family.

Wingspan of **Dreamy Duskywing** up to 1½ inches. Forewings short and rounded. Upperside forewing gray with two dark gray chainlike bands, black near base. Hindwing brown with two rows of spots. Habitat forest edges, gardens, and other open areas. Breeding resident with one brood. Flight March–June. Rare, scattered throughout the Interior Highlands.

Larva pale green, covered with small white dots, heart appears dorsally as a thin green stripe. Host plants members of the willow family.

A

B

A   Juvenal's Duskywing   *Erynnis juvenalis juvenalis*

Upperside, Logan County

Wingspan up to 1⅞ inches. Upperside ♂ forewing gray with white spots; ♀ gray and brown with more contrast, white spots. Underside hindwing has two white spots near apex. Habitat forest edges, gardens, and other open areas. Breeding resident with one brood. Flight March–June. Common statewide.

Larva green to yellow-green, markings similar to other duskywings. Head orange-brown, each side with three orange spots. Host plants members of the oak family.

B   Horace's Duskywing   *Erynnis horatius*

Upperside, Washington County

Wingspan up to 1⅞ inches. Upperside ♂ forewing dark brown with a few white spots; ♀ has contrasting brown pattern with larger white spots. Wings have brown fringe. Underside hindwing brown with pale spots, but not near the apex as in Juvenal's. Habitat open areas such as forest edges and gardens. Breeding resident with several broods. Flight March–October. Common statewide.

Larva light blue-green, very similar to Juvenal's. Host plants members of the oak family.

C   Funereal Duskywing   *Erynnis funeralis*

Upperside, Logan County

Wingspan up to 1¾ inches. Forewing narrow and pointed. Upperside black, forewing with contrasting brown and gray pattern. Hindwing fringe white. Habitat gardens, forest edges, and other open areas. Breeding resident with several broods. Flight June–September. Uncommon statewide.

Larva light green with marking similar to other duskywings, head tan or brown with three yellow-orange patches on each side. Host plants Black Locust, vetch, and other legumes.

A

B

C

A   Wild Indigo Duskywing   *Erynnis baptisiae*
Upperside, Randolph County

Wingspan up to 1⅝ inches. Upperside forewing with contrasting pattern of black and brown, darker at base, with small white transparent spots. Hindwing brown with pale bar in middle of wing, pale spots along outer margin. Habitat gardens and other open areas. Breeding resident with several broods. Flight June–September. Uncommon statewide.

Larva yellow-green with markings similar to other duskywings, head black and mottled with orange. Host plants wild indigo and Crown Vetch.

B   Common Checkered-Skipper   *Pyrgus communis*
Upperside, Logan County

Wingspan up to 1½ inches. Upperside checkered black and white, body and wing bases have bluish-gray hairs, checkered fringe; ♀ has more black. Underside hindwing white with tan bands. Habitat nearly all open areas, needs some bare ground and low-growing plants. Breeding resident with several broods. Flight June–November. Common statewide.

Larva is light green, covered with short, fine white hairs and tiny white dots, weak cream stripes, green heart line visible. Black head covered with white hairs. Collar reddish brown. Host plants members of the mallow family.

C   Common Sootywing   *Pholisora catullus*
Upperside, Washington County

Wingspan up to 1⅜ inches. Upperside glossy dark brown or black with small white spots on forewings; ♀ has more spots, including some on the hindwing. Habitat nearly all open, disturbed areas. Breeding resident with several broods. Flight April–September. Local, uncommon statewide.

Larva is pale green, with or without yellow stripes, covered with tiny yellow dots and fine hairs, head black with white hairs. Larva makes a leaf shelter and feeds at night. Host plant lamb's quarters.

A

B

C

A   Swarthy Skipper   *Nastra lherminier*
Upperside, Conway County

Wingspan up to 1⅛ inches. Upperside dark brown. Underside dull yellow-brown, making lighter veins stand out. Habitat open grassy areas. Breeding resident with two broods. Flight May–October. Rare to uncommon statewide, easily overlooked.

Larva is green with dorsal dark green stripe, head tan with reddish brown markings. Larva lives in a rolled leaf shelter. Host plant Little Bluestem.

B   Clouded Skipper   *Lerema accius*
Underside, Logan County

Wingspan up to 1¾ inches. Upperside brown; ♂ forewing has black stigma, ♀ has white spots. Underside most often seen. Hindwing dark brown, frosted with purple, vertical dark brown band in center of wing. Habitat forest edges and clearings. Breeding resident with two broods. Flight April–November, most often seen late summer through fall. Uncommon to common statewide.

Larva is green with dorsal whitish cast, white head with black markings. Host plants Eastern Gama Grass (*Tripsacum dactyloides*), Johnson grass, and other weedy grasses.

C   Least Skipper   *Ancyloxypha numitor*
Underside, Craighead County

Wingspan up to 1⅛ inches. Little skipper with weak flight. Upperside orange with black margins ; ♀ has thin black stigma; hindwing orange with black margin. Underside forewing black with orange costa and apex, hindwing orange. Habitat wet, open grassy areas. Breeding resident with several broods. Flight May–October. Uncommon to common statewide; most common skipper in the Delta and Crowley's Ridge.

Larva is green, with four pairs of abdominal white wax glands above the legs (subventral). As the larva spins a cocoon, the wax becomes part of the walls of the cocoon, and some wax will cover the surface of the pupa inside. Head round, tan or brown, circled with white or tan, darker in the center. Host plants bluegrass, rice cutgrass, and other grasses.

A

B

C

A   Fiery Skipper   *Hylephila phyleus*
Underside, Logan County

Wingspan up to 1½ inches. Very small and fast. Sexually dimorphic. Antennae short. ♂ upperside yellow-orange with black-toothed wing margins, black stigma; underside yellow-orange with small black spots. ♀ upperside has more black, underside has larger spots. Habitat gardens and other open areas. Breeding resident with two broods. Flight May–November. Spring numbers usually low, then pick up in summer, but vary yearly. Common statewide.

Larva variable: often brown with dark dorsal stripe, head black with two brown lines. Host plants grasses, mainly crabgrass and Bermuda grass. Females readily lay eggs on the lawn, but the dark larvae with black heads make a nest at the base of the host, so no worries about the lawnmower.

B   Leonard's Skipper   *Hesperia leonardus leonardus*
Underside, Conway County

Wingspan up to 1¾ inches. Conspicuous skipper. Upperside black with orange. Underside deep reddish brown with band of bright white spots. Habitat gardens and other open areas. Colonist status unclear. Flight August–October. Irregular emigrant in low numbers, has been seen in scattered locations from north to central Arkansas.

Larva tan with dark brown head. Host plants Little Bluestem and grama grass.

C   Cobweb Skipper   *Hesperia metea licinus*
Underside, Faulkner County

Wingspan up to 1⅜ inches. Upperside dark brown with some orange, forewing costal margin whitish. Underside dark brown with white chevron band and whitish veins, creating a "cobweb" appearance. Some individuals of this variable skipper may be unmarked. Habitat open grassy areas. Breeding resident with one brood. Flight April–May. Locally rare to common, mainly central and western Arkansas.

Larva is brown to brownish black. Host plants Big and Little Bluestem.

A

B

C

A   Meske's Skipper   *Hesperia meskei meskei*
Underside, Ashley County

Wingspan up to 1½ inches. Upperside dark brown with orange bands. Underside bright yellow-orange, hindwing spot band faint or absent. Habitat open, sandy pinewoods. Breeding resident with two broods. Flight April–October; seen mainly late summer to fall. Isolated and locally rare in the Ozarks, Ouachitas, and Coastal Plain.

Larva is grayish brown with brown or black head. Host plants grasses.

B   Tawny-edged Skipper   *Polites themistocles*
Upperside, Craighead County

Wingspan up to 1½ inches. Upperside dark brown with orange costa; ♂ has thick black stigma. Underside dull brown, forewing with orange leading edge. Habitat forest edges, gardens, and other open areas. Breeding resident with two broods. Flight May–October. Common statewide.

Larva is brown, speckled with white, head black. Host plants grasses.

C   Southern Broken-Dash   *Wallengrenia otho otho*
Underside, Craighead County

Wingspan up to 1⅜ inches. Upperside mostly brown on both sexes; ♂ forewing has orange costa and broken black stigma, ♀ has orange spots. Underside reddish orange; hindwing has light spot band shaped like a 3. Habitat moist woodland edges. Breeding resident with two broods. Flight May–October. Uncommon to common statewide.

Larva dark brown and speckled, head and collar black. Host plants grasses.

D   Northern Broken-Dash   *Wallengrenia egeremet*
Underside, Craighead County

Wingspan up to 1⅜ inches. Similar to Southern Broken-Dash, but underside is dull, dark brown to purple brown, with a lighter spot band. Habitat moist open areas. Breeding resident with two broods. Flight June–September. Uncommon statewide.

Larva similar to Southern Broken-Dash. Host plants grasses.

A

B

C

D

A   **Sachem**   *Atalopedes campestris huron*
Underside, Logan County

Wingspan up to 1⅝ inches. One of our most widespread skippers, a garden constant. Upperside ♂ forewing yellow-orange, brown borders, large black stigma, ♀ forewing yellow-orange or darker with two square transparent spots. Underside ♂ usually dull orange, ♀ brown with pale arrow-shaped spot band pointing outward. Habitat disturbed open areas. Breeding resident with several broods. Flight May–September. Common statewide.

Larva is dark green with tiny black dots and black head. Host plants Bermuda grass, crabgrass, and other grasses.

B   **Little Glassywing**   *Pompeius verna verna*
Underside, Craighead County

Wingspan up to 1½ inches. Upperside blackish brown; forewing has square transparent (glassy) white spot near center of wing, and a few other glassy spots. Male forewing has black stigma. Underside brown; hindwing has purple sheen and a faint spot band. Habitat moist grassy areas near woodlands. Breeding resident with several broods. Flight May–September. Rare to uncommon statewide.

Larva is light green with dark green dorsal line and two black spots near the rear, head black. Host plants grasses, primarily purple top grass.

C   **Delaware Skipper**   *Anatrytone logan logan*
Underside, Sharp County

Wingspan up to 1⅝ inches. Bright yellow-orange. Upperside outer margins and veins black, forewing with black bar at end of cell. Underside unmarked. Habitat damp, grassy areas. Breeding resident with two broods. Flight June–September. Uncommon to common statewide.

Larva blue-green with black crescent on rear end, white head circled with tan or black with three vertical stripes of the same color. Host plants grasses, including bluestem.

A

B

C

A   Byssus Skipper   *Problema byssus kumskaka*

1) Upperside, Faulkner County
2) Underside, Scott County

Wingspan up to 1⅞ inches. Variable. Upperside ♂ orange with black borders
and black forewing cell-end bar; ♀ mostly black with some orange. Underside
♂ hindwing dull yellow-orange to orange-brown with pale patch; ♀ orange to
reddish brown with pale spot band. Habitat prairies and wet woodland edges.
Breeding resident with one brood. Flight May–September. Local; uncommon to
common throughout the Interior Highlands.

Larva is bluish green. White head encircled with black with three black vertical
stripes. Host plants grasses including plume grass and Eastern Gama Grass
(*Tripsacum dactyloides*).

B   Zabulon Skipper   *Poanes zabulon*

1) Underside ♂, Craighead County
2) Underside ♀, Craighead County

Wingspan up to 1⅜ inches. Sexually dimorphic. Upperside ♂ yellow-orange
with black borders and forewing cell-end bar, ♀ brown with a few white spots.
Underside ♂ yellow; hindwing with brown base and wing margin, a yellow spot
is within brown base. Underside ♀ purple-brown, hindwing outer margins pur-
ple-gray, costal margin white-edged near apex, darker brown patch in center.
Habitat open moist woodlands, parks, and gardens. Breeding resident with two
broods. Flight April–September. Uncommon to common statewide.

Larva is greenish brown. Brown head is covered with fine hairs (pubescent).
Host plants grasses.

A 1

A 2

B 1

B 2

A   Hobomok Skipper   *Poanes hobomok hobomok*
Upperside, Washington County

Wingspan up to 1⅜ inches. Upperside yellow-orange with dark brown borders. Underside hindwing yellow orange, ♀ orange, with a large yellow postmedian patch. The ♀ has a second form, "pocahontas," upperside forewing brownish-purple with a few white spots, underside with purple-brown pattern. Habitat open moist woodlands. Breeding resident with one brood. Flight May–July. Rare to uncommon, mostly known from the Ozarks.

Larva is brownish green, brown pubescent head. Host plants grasses, especially panic grass.

B   Yehl Skipper   *Poanes yehl*
Underside, Lee County

Wingspan up to 1¼ inches. Upperside orange with black borders, ♂ forewing has stigma, ♀ black at base. Underside ♂ hindwing dull orange, ♀ brown, with a band of 3–5 pale spots divided by a pale streak. Habitat open areas in moist or swampy woods. Breeding resident with two broods. Flight May–October. Rare to uncommon statewide in proper habitat.

Larva is tan, speckled with green, covered with fine hair, dark green dorsal stripe, pale lateral stripes, and brown pubescent head. Host plant giant cane.

C   Broad-winged Skipper   *Poanes viator zizaniae*
Underside, Mississippi County

Wingspan up to 2⅛ inches. Upperside dark brown, ♂ forewing with orange spots, ♀ with white spots. Underside brownish orange with a pale yellow-orange streak extending from base across a row of yellow-orange spots. Habitat wetlands with tall grass. Breeding resident with several broods. Flight May–October, mostly seen in summer. Rare to locally common, mostly known from wetlands in the Delta.

Larva is tan with white lateral stripes; head has a black vertical stripe. Host plants common reed, wild rice, and sedges.

A

B

C

A   Duke's Skipper   *Euphyes dukesi*
Underside, Craighead County

Wingspan up to 1¾ inches. Upperside black; forewing with orange leading edge on ♂, two white spots on ♀. Underside forewing black in center, hindwing brownish orange with a yellow streak extending from base to wing margin. Habitat shady swamps, marshes, and ditches. Breeding resident with two broods. Flight June–September. Local; rare to uncommon throughout the Coastal Plain.

Larva is light green with tiny black dots, thoracic collar white and black; head has white-and-brown-striped pattern with a white-edged black spot in the center, all characteristics of the genus. Host plants sedges.

B   Dun Skipper   *Euphyes vestris metacomet*
Underside, Craighead County

Wingspan up to 1⅛ inches. Upperside brownish black, ♂ forewing with black stigma, ♀ with two white spots. Underside plain dark brown. Habitat open riparian areas, moist woodland edges or prairies. Breeding resident with two broods. Flight May–October. Uncommon to common statewide.

Larva light green with tiny black dots, thoracic collar white and black; head has white-and-brown-striped pattern with a white-edged black spot in the center, all characteristics of the genus. Host plants sedges.

C   Dusted Skipper   *Atrytonopsis hianna hianna*
Underside, Faulkner County

Wingspan up to 1⅝ inches. White face, upper half of eyes edged with white. Upperside brown with white forewing dots. Underside brown, gray outer margins, brown fringe, hindwing with a white spot at base. Habitat fields, prairies, and barrens. Breeding resident with one brood. Flight April–May. Local, uncommon statewide.

Larva dull green to tan, often with a pink cast, covered with fine hairs. Dark brown pubescent head. Host plants Big and Little Bluestem Grass.

A

B

C

The **Roadside-Skippers,** genus *Amblyscirtes*, can be difficult to identify in the field. Seven species occur in Arkansas. They are dark in color, fast fliers, and stay close to the ground. One feature they all share is checkered wing fringe. Larvae are greenish; their heads are pale with vertical stripes and rimmed with a dark color. Larvae create aerial nests when feeding, and full-grown larvae overwinter on the ground in a nest made with grass blades.

A   Linda's Roadside-Skipper   *Amblyscirtes linda*

Upperside, Washington County

Wingspan up to 1⅜ inches. Upperside dark brown; forewing has tiny white spot. Underside dark brown, hindwing speckled with gray, with a whitish gray post-median spot band. Habitat moist woodlands. Breeding resident with two broods. Flight April–September. Local, rare, known from the northern part of the state. This butterfly was first described to science from Faulkner County in 1943.

Larva is pale bluish green, head white with brown vertical stripes. Host plant broadleaf uniola.

B   Lace-winged Roadside-Skipper   *Amblyscirtes aesculapius*

Underside, Lee County

Wingspan up to 1½ inches. Upperside dark brown, forewing with white spots. Underside brown, hindwing has distinctive "lacy" white cobweb pattern. Fringes vividly checkered black and white. Habitat riparian areas with cane. Breeding resident with two broods. Flight April–September. Local, rare to uncommon statewide in canebrakes.

Larva is grayish green, head light tan with brown stripes. Host plants giant cane and switch cane.

C   Common Roadside-Skipper   *Amblyscirtes vialis*

Upperside, Washington County

Wingspan up to 1½ inches. Upperside black with a few tiny white spots on forewing apex. Underside black; forewing apex and hindwing margins are frosted with gray. Habitat open areas near woods, often roadsides, hence the name. Breeding resident with two broods. Flight April–August. Rare to locally common statewide.

Larva is whitish green, head gray with dark gray stripes. Host plants grasses.

A

B

C

A   Bell's Roadside-Skipper   *Amblyscirtes belli*

Underside, Logan County

Wingspan up to 1¼ inches. Upperside dark black-brown, forewing has several white spots. Underside dark brown; all but forewing apex is speckled with gray scales with several white spots; hindwing spots may form a band. Habitat open riparian areas, urban areas, and gardens. Breeding resident with two broods. Flight late March–September. Uncommon to common, nearly statewide except southern Delta.

Larva is green, head white with brown vertical stripe. Host plants broadleaf uniola and Johnson grass.

B   Ocola Skipper   *Panoquina ocola*

Underside, Logan County

Wingspan up to 1⅝ inches. Forewings elongated, narrow, and held down at rest. Look closely for a stripe along the abdomen. Underside dark brown, often with a purple sheen. Hindwing has a faint spot band near the middle. Habitat moist open areas such as gardens, fields, and forest edges. Colonist status unclear. Flight June–November. Regular emigrant in low numbers, has been seen in scattered locations throughout the state.

Larva is green with a thin white stripe below the spiracles, and a green head. Host plants grasses.

C   Brazilian Skipper   *Calpodes ethlius*

1) Upperside, Washington County
2) Larva, Greene County

Wingspan up to 2⅜ inches. Large, stout skipper with long, narrow forewings. Upperside dark brown with large white spots on both wings. Underside reddish brown, hindwing has three translucent white spots, forewing two. Infrequent colonist in low numbers. Habitat residential gardens and wetlands where cannas grow. Flight August–October. Locally rare to locally uncommon wherever host grows.

Larva is green, translucent, and the white lines of the tracheal system (from the spiracles inward) are visible. Larva folds host plant leaves to create nest. Host plants tropical cannas (grown from bulbs). Bulbs are usually available for purchase at most garden centers fall and spring. Gardeners be warned: folded leaf nests indicate these skippers' presence, and one might think of some other pest at first and take hasty actions to eradicate them.

A

B

C 1

C 2

Additional Resident Skippers to Watch For:

Mottled Duskywing, *Erynnis martialis*, has a wingspan up to 1⅝ inches. Upperside has strong mottled pattern of gray, black, and brown. Many fresh individuals have a purple sheen. Males may be observed engaging in hilltopping behavior. Habitat forest edges and other open areas. Breeding resident with several broods. Flight May–July. Local, uncommon statewide. Larva is similar to other duskywings. Host plant New Jersey tea.

The **Southern Skipperling,** *Copaeodes minima*, has a wingspan up to ⅞ inches. This is the smallest skipper, bright orange on both sides; upperside forewing has narrow black border, ♂ thin black stigma. Habitat open fields. Breeding resident with several broods. Flight March–October. Rare to uncommon; southern Coastal Plain, has strayed northeast. Larva is green with a dark dorsal stripe divided by a light line, several pale stripes, and green head. Red-tipped pointed "tail." Host plant Bermuda grass.

Peck's Skipper, *Polites peckius*, has a wingspan up to 1¼ inches. Upperside black with orange at forewing base and spots; central spot extends outward. Underside brown with large yellow patches; the central spot in the patch near the wing margins extends outward. Habitat open areas. This butterfly may be a temporary colonist. Flight May–October. Rare to uncommon, known from Washington, Benton, and Carroll counties, more common in the northern part of the United States. Larva is speckled, blackish brown, with a dark dorsal stripe and a black head with faint white lines, very similar to other *Polites*. Host plants grasses.

The **Crossline Skipper,** *Polites origenes*, has a wingspan up to 1½ inches. Upperside dark brown with a few orange spots; ♂ forewing has orange costa and long thin black stigma. Underside brownish yellow. Hindwing has pale, nearly straight spot band near wing margin. Variations may have faint spot band. Habitat dry, open areas. Breeding resident with two broods. Flight May–October. Uncommon to common statewide. Larva is brown and speckled with white, with a black head. Host plants grasses.

The **Whirlabout,** *Polites vibex vibex*, has a wingspan up to 1½ inches, and is named for "whirling" flight. Sexually dimorphic. Upperside ♂ yellowish orange, black stigma and patches, forewing orange with black borders; ♀ dark brown, forewing has a few pale spots. Underside ♂ yellow-orange, ♀ brown with olive-green shading. Hindwing has two broken rows of dark brown spots that roughly form the corners of a square. Habitat disturbed areas. Breeding status unclear, may be a regular colonist. Flight May–October. Rare to uncommon in the southern part of the state, also sighted occasionally in the Ouachita Mountains and Arkansas River Valley. Larva color varies from green to purple. Head is brown or black with pale spots and two vertical stripes near the top. Host plants grasses, including Bermuda grass and crabgrass.

The **Arogos Skipper,** *Atrytone arogos iowa*, has a wingspan up to 1⅛ inches. Upperside yellow with black wing margins. ♀ margins broader; forewing has long black basal streak. Underside yellowish orange, hindwing fringe and veins whitish. Habitat high-quality prairie. Breeding resident with one brood. Flight May–June. This is an extremely local and rare skipper in Franklin County. Larva is slender and bluish green. Tan head is circled with red and has three reddish brown facial stripes. Host plant Big Bluestem.

The **Dion Skipper,** *Euphyes dion dion*, has a wingspan up to 1¼ inches. Sexually dimorphic upperside; ♂ orange with dark brown borders and black stigma, ♀ brown with some orange spots on forewing; both sexes have two orange streaks on hindwing extending from the base, but the upper streak does not cross the entire wing. Underside hindwing dull reddish-orange with two pale orange streaks. Habitat wetlands. Breeding resident with two broods. Flight June–September. Locally uncommon to locally common statewide in proper habitat. Larva is similar to other members of the *Euphyes* genus. Host plants sedges.

The **Pepper and Salt Skipper,** *Amblyscirtes hegon*, is a roadside-skipper with a wingspan up to 1⅛ inch. Upperside brown with white spots. Underside has grayish green shading with several white spots; hindwing typically has a white postmedian spot band. Habitat open riparian areas, glades, and woodland edges. Breeding resident with two broods. Flight April–July. Local, rare statewide. Larva is greenish white with dark dorsal stripe and tan head with triangular stripe in center. Host plants broadleaf uniola and other grasses.

The **Carolina Roadside-Skipper,** *Amblyscirtes carolina*, has a wingspan up to 1¼ inches. Upperside dark brown, forewing with yellow spots. Underside dull yellow with dark reddish brown spots. Pale abdomen has dark brown spots. Habitat riparian areas with cane. Breeding resident with one brood. Flight April–September. Locally rare, known from the Ozarks and Delta. Larva is grayish green, head light tan with brown stripes. Host plants giant cane and switch cane.

The **Dusky Roadside-Skipper,** *Amblyscirtes alternata*, has a wingspan up to 1 inch, forewings pointed. Upperside blackish brown, faint-to-absent white forewing spots. Underside black, dusted with gray. Habitat open pinewoods. Breeding resident with two broods. Flight March–August. Rare to uncommon in southern Arkansas. Larva is greenish white, head white with brown lateral stripes and three pale facial stripes. Host plants Big and Little Bluestem and other grasses.

The **Eufala Skipper,** *Lerodea eufala*, has a wingspan up to 1⅜ inches. Upperside brown, forewing with white spots. Underside tan, either plain or with a few faint spots. Habitat open areas. Breeding resident with two broods. Flight June–October. Uncommon, nearly statewide. Larva is greenish, white head circled with brown and brown vertical stripe in center. Larva feeds at a slower rate during the winter instead of creating a hibernaculum. Host plants Bermuda, Johnson, and other grasses.

The **Yucca Giant-Skipper**, *Megathymus yuccae yuccae*, has a wingspan up to 3⅛ inches. Large, blackish brown. Upperside has cream-yellow bands. Underside with frosted gray margins; hindwing has large white spot on costa. Habitat fields and pinewoods where yuccas grow. Breeding resident with one brood. Flight spring, mainly April–May. Locally rare in the Ouachitas and Coastal Plain. Larva is white with a black head; the first instar is red. Host plants yuccas.

Additional Skippers That Occasionally Stray into Arkansas:

> **Outis Skipper,** *Cogia outis*
> **Sickle-winged Skipper,** *Eantis tamenund*
> **Zarucco Duskywing,** *Erynnis zarucco*
> **Tropical Checkered-Skipper,** *Pyrgus oileus*
> **Desert Checkered-Skipper,** *Pyrgus philetas*
> **Northern White-Skipper,** *Heliopetes ericetorum*
> **Nysa Roadside-Skipper,** *Amblyscirtes nysa*

Swallowtails (Family Papilionidae)

Swallowtails are some of the largest, most popular, and most familiar butterflies. Almost all our swallowtails can be seen spring, summer, and fall. These butterflies are named for the elongated "tails" on their hindwings, resembling the long tails of swallows. The tails distract predators away from more vital parts of the body. If a predator does attack, usually only a tail is lost. Swallowtails are fun to watch, from the swift, erratic flight of Pipevine Swallowtails to the graceful flight of Giant and Tiger Swallowtails.

Swallowtails are easily attracted to gardens and are generally easy to identify. Males can often be observed mud-puddling. Males search for females by patrolling or perching. Unmated swallowtails may be observed hilltopping.

Although the larvae of each species are different in color, behavior, and host plant, a trait they share is a long, fleshy, Y-shaped organ called the osmeterium. When a larva is threatened, this organ juts out from behind the head and emits a foul odor. This odor is produced by isobutyric and 2-methyl-butyric acid in all swallowtails but the Pipevine, whose odor is produced by two sesquiterpenes. The odors are enhanced by other acids, esters, and terpenes in all swallowtails.

Swallowtail chrysalises are usually brown or green for camouflage, often the color of the plant or wooden surface they choose. They are attached by a silk button at the bottom, and held in place by a silk girdle. All our swallowtails overwinter as a chrysalis. Spring adults are usually smaller than summer adults.

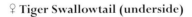

♀ Tiger Swallowtail (underside)

A   Pipevine Swallowtail   *Battus philenor*

1) Upperside, Logan County
2) Larva, Washington County

Wingspan up to 5¼ inches. Upperside black; hindwings a shimmering, iridescent blue-green. Underside hindwing has a row of orange spots inside a large metallic blue area. Female iridescence is subdued; males are much brighter. Habitat open, disturbed areas, woodland openings. This butterfly has an erratic, nervous-looking flight, even when nectaring. Breeding resident, several broods. Flight March–November. Common statewide.

Larva dark chocolate brown with fleshy, paired tubercles; two dorsal rows of tubercles reddish orange. Host plants are members of the pipe vine family *(Aristolochia)*. Pipe vines are toxic, so consumption makes the larvae and adults toxic. Other butterflies mimic the Pipevine Swallowtail, even those that are tailless and belong to different families: Spicebush Swallowtail, female Eastern Tiger Swallowtail, Black Swallowtail, Red-spotted Purple, and female Diana.

B   Zebra Swallowtail   *Eurytides marcellus*

1) Upperside, Logan County
2) Larva, black form, Logan County

Wingspan up to 4 inches. Unmistakable greenish white and black zebra-stripe markings. Underside hindwing has a red median stripe. Spring form small with short tails, summer form large with long tails. Sometimes called "kite" swallowtails due to tails and angular wing shape. The proboscis is shorter than that of other swallowtails, so it must take nectar from flowers with shorter floral tubes. Habitat forested areas; adults nectar in open areas near forests. Breeding resident with several broods. Flight March–September. Common statewide, seen more often in spring and early summer.

Larva has two forms: green form has thin yellow cross bands and a wide black band at the thoracic hump; the black form has yellow and white cross bands. Larva is thicker at thoracic hump. Host plant pawpaw.

A 1

A 2

B 1

B 2

Black Swallowtail   *Papilio polyxenes asterius*

1) Upperside ♂, Logan County
2) Underside, Logan County
3) Larva, Logan County
4) Chrysalis, Logan County

Wingspan up to 4½ inches. Upperside forewing black with two rows of yellow spots; hindwing with red-orange eyespot enclosing a black "pupil" near tails. Females have large blue area on upperside hindwing that males lack. Yellow-spotted abdomen. Habitat open areas. Breeding resident, several broods. Flight April–September. Common statewide.

Full-grown larva green with black bands on each segment with yellow-orange spots. First instar larvae resemble bird droppings. Host plants members of the carrot family, especially parsley, dill, fennel, parsnip, and Queen Anne's Lace.

The **Ozark Swallowtail,** *Papilio joanae,* is incredibly difficult to distinguish from the Black Swallowtail as an adult, with roughly the same size and flight period. The best field mark to use is the "pupil" in the eyespot near the tails on the upperside, because it touches the edge of the wing. Habitat cedar glades and woodlands. Breeding status unclear. Flight April–September. Rare and local in the Ozarks. Larva is similar to that of the Black Swallowtail. Host plants meadow parsnip, Yellow Pimpernel, Golden Alexander, and others.

1

2

3

4

Eastern Tiger Swallowtail   *Papilio glaucus glaucus*

1) Upperside ♂, Logan County
2) Upperside ♀, dark form, Logan County
3) Upperside ♀, yellow form, Logan County
4) Larva, Logan County

Wingspan up to 6½ inches. Summer adults often rival the size of Giant Swallowtails. Males are yellow with black tiger stripes. Females are dimorphic with most in Arkansas being the dark form, underside tiger stripe is visible for identification. The black female form mimics the Pipevine Swallowtail. Habitat deciduous forests, forest edges, gardens, meadows, and river valleys. Breeding resident with several broods. Flight March–October. Common statewide.

Larva is smooth and green, with two small yellow eyespots on thoracic hump and a yellow band. Larva usually turns brown just before pupating. Host plants a variety of trees including Black Cherry, cottonwood, and Tulip-Tree.

1

2

3

4

Spicebush Swallowtail   *Papilio troilus troilus*

1) Upperside ♂ , Logan County
2) Upperside ♀ , Logan County
3) Underside, Logan County
4) Larva, Logan County

Wingspan up to 5 inches. Males and females sexually dimorphic, but both essentially black with a row of white spots on top and bottom. Male hindwings upperside have a large blue-green area, female hindwings have small amount of iridescent blue. Undersides of hindwings have a brilliant blue area surrounded by orange-red spots; notice lack of one orange spot on the orange band near the middle. Habitat woodlands and open fields. Mimics the Pipevine Swallowtail. Breeding resident with several broods. Flight March–October. Common statewide.

Larva striking: smooth and green on top, yellowish white laterally. Abdominal segments also have longitudinal rows of blue spots. Thoracic hump has two pairs of black-ringed orange eyespots, larger eyespots with black circle inside, smaller eyespots without black. Larva folds leaf shelters for additional protection. Larva usually turns golden yellow-orange or brown before pupating. Host plants spicebush and Sassafras.

1

2

3

4

Giant Swallowtail   *Papilio cresphontes*

1) Upperside, Logan County
2) Larva, Logan County
3) Underside, mating pair, Logan County

Wingspan up to 6½ inches. One of the largest butterflies in North America. Upperside forewings and hindwings brownish black with easily recognized yellow spot bands. Tails with yellow spots. Underside mostly yellow. Habitat open areas, including forested areas, river valleys, towns. Breeding resident with two broods. Flight April–October. Common statewide.

Larva is mottled brown with a creamy white dorsal saddle in the middle and white blotches. It resembles a bird dropping and is often called the "orange dog." Host plants members of the citrus family, including Prickly Ash, Wafer Ash, and Trifoliate Orange.

Additional Swallowtails That Occasionally Stray into and/or Form Temporary Colonies in Arkansas:

The tailless **Polydamas Swallowtail,** *Battus polydamas,* bred in the state in the 1960s. Despite the abundance of its larval host, pipe vines, this southern swallowtail appears to only be an infrequent colonist.
Palamedes Swallowtail, *Papilio palamedes*

1

2

3

*The butterfly counts not months but moments,
and has time enough.*

—*Rabindranath Tagore*

Whites and Sulphurs (Family Pieridae)

Whites and sulphurs are widespread and familiar butterflies. They are often the first butterflies seen in the spring, and last in the fall and winter. They bask with their wings closed and turned sideways toward the sun. Some members of this family can be seen year round. All these butterflies are attracted to gardens and fairly easy to identify, with the exception of white females and Orange Sulphur-Clouded Sulphur hybrids. The yellow pigmentation in sulphurs is produced mostly by nitrogen.

Males are often observed mud-puddling and patrolling for mates. It's sometimes difficult for the human eye to distinguish male Clouded Sulphurs and Orange Sulphurs, but it's not hard for the females of these two species. We can't see the ultraviolet light they reflect. Orange Sulphurs reflect more ultraviolet light than Clouded Sulphurs, so females of each species can pick the appropriate mate. There are a few exceptions to this rule. Male hybrids of the two species do not reflect ultraviolet light, and females can thus be fooled, and females freshly emerged from their chrysalises may be too weak to reject the wrong species.

The eggs of white butterflies turn red a few hours after they are laid to deter other females from laying eggs on the same plant. Since the host plants are small, they can only support one caterpillar. Too many caterpillars at once may result in cannibalism. The host plants of this family are mustards (whites) and legumes (sulphurs). Some of these caterpillars are pests of crops and gardens, the most notorious being the caterpillar of the Cabbage White.

All chrysalises of this family attach to a plant or wooden surface with a silk button and are held in place by a silk girdle. Most whites overwinter as a chrysalis. Clouded and Orange Sulphurs typically spend the winter as chrysalises, but Orange Sulphurs may be seen flying on warm winter days. Other sulphurs overwinter as adults. Winter and spring adults are usually smaller and darker than summer adults. This helps warm their flight muscles quickly in cold temperatures.

Cloudless Sulphur, freshly emerged from chrysalis

A   Checkered White   *Pontia protodice*
Upperside, Logan County

Wingspan up to 2 inches. Variable spring and summer forms. Wings have a white-and-black-checkered pattern; ♀ heavier; ♂ hindwings white. Underside ♂ checkered, ♀ has yellowish brown veins. Habitat open, dry areas such as old fields, roadsides, and vacant lots. Males patrol flat areas. Breeding resident with several broods. Flight February–September, seen most often midsummer. Uncommon to common statewide.

Larva is blue-green with lateral yellow and steel-blue stripes. Shiny black spots with setae cover the head and body. Host plants peppergrass, cabbage, and other mustards.

B   Cabbage White   *Pieris rapae*
Underside, Craighead County

Wingspan up to 2¼ inches. Upperside white with black-tipped forewings, ♂ with one black spot in the middle of the forewing, ♀ has two spots. Underside pale yellow, grayish white, greenish, or white. Habitat open and weedy areas, especially in cities and gardens, not often seen in woodlands or mountainous regions. A widespread, introduced species. Breeding resident with several broods. Flight March–December. Uncommon to common statewide.

Larva is light green with thin yellow dorsal stripe and is covered with tiny hairs and black spots. Some individuals have broken yellow spiracular stripes. Larva is considered a pest of cabbage and other mustards.

A

B

A   Falcate Orangetip   *Anthocharis midea*

1) Upperside ♂ , Logan County
2) Underside ♀ , Logan County

Wingspan up to 1¼ inches. Forewing apex curved and pointed (falcate). Sexually dimorphic; ♂ orange-tipped forewings, ♀ white. Both sexes have a small black spot on upperside forewing. Underside has marbled dark green pattern. Habitat open wet woods near streams and rivers, forest edges, ridgetops, and gardens. Breeding resident with one brood. Flight March–May. Common statewide.

Larva is green with lateral white stripes, faint blue shading, and a yellow dorsal stripe. Host plants Rock Cress, Winter Cress, Water Cress, Toothwort, and other mustards. Females have been observed laying eggs on Shepherd's Purse and Dame's Rocket, but the eggs did not hatch on these plants. The chrysalis over-winters, and the adult may not emerge for two or three years.

B   Olympia Marble   *Euchloe olympia*

Upperside, Logan County

Wingspan up to 2 inches. Upperside white with soft black shading on forewing edge. Underside has bright, simple green marbling. Habitat open areas such as glades and forest edges. Flies close to the ground, feeds on low flowers such as phlox and mustards. Breeding resident with one brood. Flight March–May. Local, rare, mostly seen in the Interior Highlands.

Larva similar to Falcate Orangetip, but there is some yellow below the white stripes and more blue shading. Host plants mustards, primarily Rock Cress.

A 1

A 2

B

A   Clouded Sulphur   *Colias philodice*

Upperside, Washington County

Wingspan up to 2¾ inches. Upperside yellow; males have solid black wing margins, female margins have yellow spots. There is a black spot in the center of the forewing, and an orange spot on the hindwing. The underside has a white-centered black spot on the forewings and two silver spots encircled with pink on the hindwings. Habitat open fields, roadsides, city gardens. Breeding resident with several broods. This butterfly may hybridize with the Orange Sulphur. Flight March–November. Common statewide, but not as common as the Orange Sulphur.

Larva is green with lateral white stripe, which may have pink to red bars. Host plants legumes.

Whitish green females, form "alba," sometimes occur due to females using nitrogen reserves to produce more fit eggs instead of producing yellow coloration. However, yellow females are preferred as mates.

B   Orange Sulphur   *Colias eurytheme*

1) Upperside, Washington County
2) Underside, Logan County

Wingspan up to 2½ inches. Upperside yellow-orange to dark orange; males have solid black wing margins, female margins have orange-yellow spots. Underside similar to Clouded Sulphur. White females also occur. White females, hybrids, and light orange sulphurs of both species are extremely difficult to tell apart. Breeding resident with several broods. Flight March–November, and may be seen all throughout the winter months if the weather is warm. Common statewide.

Larva is dark green with lateral white stripes. Host plants legumes.

A

B 1

B 2

A   Southern Dogface   *Zerene cesonia*

1) Upperside, Chicot County
2) Underside, Logan County

Wingspan up to 3 inches. Forewing tips are pointed. Called "dogface" because of the distinctive upperside dogface pattern, which can also be seen from the underside. Underside of the summer form is yellow and the fall form is darker with pink shading. Habitat open areas including pastures and woodlands. Summer breeding resident with several broods. Overwinters as an adult. Flight April–October, seen most often in fall. Rare to uncommon statewide.

Larva has two forms: green with yellow and black cross bands and a cream-to-yellow lateral stripe, or no cross bands. Host plants lead plant, prairie clover, false indigo, and other legumes.

B   Cloudless Sulphur   *Phoebis sennae eubule*

1) Underside ♀, Logan County
2) Larva, green form, Logan County

Wingspan up to 3 inches. Large, common yellow butterfly. Sexually dimorphic: ♂ bright lemon yellow, ♀ yellow, pinkish orange, or greenish white; ♀ forewing has a hollow black cell-end spot and uneven black outer margin. Undersides of both sexes have pink-rimmed silver cell-end spots on both wings; ♀ has a broken line leading to the forewing tip. Habitat nearly all open areas such as gardens, urban settings, and meadows. Adults are fond of red wildflowers such as Cardinal Flower. Summer breeding resident with several broods. Numbers are supplemented with migrants. Flight April–December. Common statewide, especially late summer through fall.

Larva has green and yellow forms. The green form shown has a lateral yellow stripe, also black tubercles and small blue dots on each side. Host plants Wild Senna and Partridge Pea.

A 1

A 2

B 1

B 2

A   Sleepy Orange   *Abaeis nicippe*

1) Underside, Logan County
2) Larva, Logan County

Wingspan up to 2 inches. Nothing sleepy about this butterfly! Variable seasonal forms and sexually dimorphic. Usually recognized on the upperside by dark orange and black outer margins (form "rosa"). Underside light to dark orange-yellow in summer, brick red in fall and winter. Habitat open woods, fields, roadsides, and watercourses. Summer breeding resident with several broods. Flight March–December. Common statewide, especially late summer through fall.

Larva is green with a lateral white and yellow stripe. Host plant Wild Senna.

B   Little Yellow   *Pyrisitia lisa*

Underside, Greene County

Wingspan up to 1¾ inches. Sexually dimorphic, some females pale yellow and white in addition to yellow. Upperside forewing apex has black border, hindwing with black border. Underside yellow, usually with some black dots, often with a round pink spot at hindwing apex. Habitat open areas such as roadsides and gardens. Summer breeding resident with several broods. Flight April–November. Common statewide, though numbers vary each year.

Larva is green with a lateral white stripe. Host plants Wild Senna and Partridge Pea.

C   Dainty Sulphur   *Nathalis iole*

Underside, Logan County

Wingspan up to 1¼ inches, the smallest sulphur. Upperside is black and yellow. Underside forewing has orange-yellow patch and black spots. Sexually dimorphic and seasonal forms. Underside hindwings usually yellow in summer, dusky green in winter and spring (form "viridis"). Habitat dry, open areas such as fields and meadows. Summer breeding resident with several broods. Adults are sometimes easy to flush when walking through weedy areas. Flight February–December, might be year round in mild winters. Common statewide, numbers vary each year.

Larva is green; it may or may not have maroon stripes. Two red bumps above the head. Host plants low-growing members of the aster family.

A 1

A 2

B

C

Additional Whites and Sulphurs That Occasionally Stray into Arkansas:

Florida White, *Appias drusilla*
Great Southern White, *Ascia monuste*
Large Orange Sulphur, *Phoebis agarithe*
Orange-barred Sulphur, *Phoebis philea*
Lyside Sulphur, *Kricogonia lyside*
Barred Yellow, *Eurema daira*
Mexican Yellow, *Eurema mexicana,* regularly wanders into Arkansas in low numbers.

Coppers, Hairstreaks, and Blues (Family Lycaenidae)

This is a family of small to tiny butterflies. They hold their wings closed when at rest, which is a pity, since some are brilliantly colored. The females have six fully developed walking legs, while the first pair of male legs is reduced. Males can often be found in large mud-puddling groups. They are fast fliers.

The larvae are sluglike, covered with short hairs called setae, and most species have variable colors and patterns. Some caterpillars are the same color as the flowers they consume. The Harvester is carnivorous and feeds on woolly aphids.

A wonderful symbiotic relationship (mutualism) is at work for many members of this family. The larvae have a special abdominal gland that secretes honeydew, a sugary liquid that attracts ants. The ants, in exchange, protect the larvae from predators and parasites. Some of the larvae even have specialized body parts they use to rub on hard surfaces and "call" the ants. Larvae leave the host plants to pupate, and the chrysalis is attached with a silk girdle and cremaster.

Hairstreaks and azures can be difficult to distinguish in the field, but the azures have their own identity crisis. The term "Spring Azure Complex" is used to describe this group because the relationships between the azures are complicated and not fully understood. The spring azure was once thought to be a variable species with several forms and subspecies, but recent research proposes several of these as full species. Enjoy and marvel at the azures rather than try to keep all variations, forms, or species straight. This is a puzzle that scientists will be working to piece together for a long time. Complex relationships like this show that we still have much to learn about our beloved butterflies and moths, and that is the fun of science!

♀ Bronze Copper (upperside)

A   Harvester   *Feniseca tarquinius*
Underside, Newton County

Wingspan up to 1¼ inches. Upperside orangish brown with black spots and broad black forewing margins. Underside reddish brown with dark spots encircled with white. Habitat riparian, usually with beech and alder present. This butterfly has a small proboscis, and can get so absorbed in feeding it lets you get close. This butterfly utilizes carnivore scat, honeydew, horse urine, and sandy areas. Breeding resident with several broods. Flight March–August. Local; rare to uncommon statewide.

Larva is variable: gray, brown, or green, with reddish or black stripes, long setae. This is our only carnivorous caterpillar, feeding on woolly aphids in association with beech and alder trees. Larvae usually covered with substances from prey. Larvae are usually found underneath the aphids and often tended by ants. The life cycle is rapid, typically ten days.

B   American Copper   *Lycaena phlaeas*
Upperside, Newton County

Wingspan up to 1¼ inches. Upperside forewings dark orange with black spots and gray margins, hindwings gray with dark orange inner margin and black spots. Underside forewings orange, with black spots, gray margin, hindwings gray, with black spots and thin orange line near wing margin. Habitat disturbed open areas. Breeding resident with several broods. Flight April–September. Uncommon, usually seen in the northern part of the state.

Larva is green with short pinkish hairs, dorsal heart line may be visible. Body is covered with tiny white dots known as "mushroom" setae. Late instars spend the day concealed in leaf litter, and feed at night. The larva overwinters. Host plants Sheep Sorrel and other docks.

A

B

A   Bronze Copper   *Lycaena hyllus*

1) Upperside ♂, Mississippi County
2) Underside ♂, Poinsett County

Wingspan up to 1¼ inches. Sexually dimorphic. Upperside ♀ two-toned: forewings orange with brown margin, hindwings brown with orange margin, black spots. Upperside ♂ iridescent purplish brown with orange border on hindwings, but with fewer black spots than ♀. Underside forewings orange with whitish gray border, hindwings white with orange outer band, black spots on both wings. Habitat wet open areas like streams, swamps, rivers. Breeding resident with several broods. Flight April–November. Local, rare to uncommon, numbers decrease if flooding occurs. Eastern Arkansas is part of the southern periphery of this butterfly's range. Most known colonies are from the Delta and Crowley's Ridge near the Mississippi River. This is a species of special concern.

Larva is greenish yellow, green dorsal heart line visible, covered with tiny white dots ("mushroom" setae). Host plants Water Dock and Curled Dock.

B   Great Purple Hairstreak   *Atlides halesus*

1) Upperside, Washington County
2) Underside, Washington County

Wingspan up to 1¼ inches. Unmistakable large and beautiful hairstreak. Upperside iridescent blue with black wing margins; rarely seen. Undersides black with red basal spots. Abdomen is blue above and red below. Habitat wooded areas with mistletoe, but sometimes this butterfly is found several miles away. These butterflies usually nectar singly on flowers, and usually perch at high levels. Breeding resident with several broods. Flight March–October. Uncommon to locally common statewide in its preferred habitat.

Larva bright green and covered with tiny yellowish hairs and a diamond-shaped mark above the head. This caterpillar is often heavily parasitized by wasps and flies. Host plant mistletoe. Chrysalises are sheltered under leaf litter or bark at the base of mistletoe tree hosts.

A 1

A 2

B 1

B 2

A   Henry's Elfin   *Callophrys henrici turneri*

Underside, Washington County

Wingspan up to 1⅛ inches. Dark brown and tailed. Male has no stigma upperside. Underside forewing has a nearly straight white line near wing margin, hindwing margin frosted with some white. Habitat open areas such as forest edges. Adults take nectar from Wild Plum, Redbud, and other spring blossoms. Breeding resident with one brood. Flight February–May. Local, uncommon to common statewide.

Larva variable in color, can be green, red, or maroon with yellow or red lateral stripes, with dorsal oblique yellow-green stripes creating a sawtooth pattern. Pupa overwinters. Host plants Redbud, American Holly, buckthorn, and blueberries.

The **Frosted Elfin,** *Callophrys irus hadros,* has a wingspan up to 1¼ inches. Similar to Henry's Elfin, it is dark brown with short tails. Underside forewing line uneven, hindwing has broad frosted margin with black spot near tail. Habitat open areas that are sandy, rocky, scrub, burned, and also woodland edges. Breeding resident with one brood. Flight March–April. This locally rare to uncommon butterfly occurs in western Coastal Plain and Ouachita Mountains, and is a species of special concern. Larva is pale green with white lateral stripes and short white hairs. Host plants wild indigo and lupine.

B   Eastern Pine Elfin   *Callophrys niphon niphon*

1) Upperside, Washington County
2) Underside, Washington County

Wingspan up to 1¼ inches. Brown and tailless with checkered fringe. Upperside orangish brown. Underside has eye-catching pattern of reddish brown, black, and grayish white. Hindwing has black crescents above gray outer margin. Habitat pine barrens, pine forests, and mixed forests. Breeding resident with one brood. Flight March–June. Common statewide.

Larva is green with white dorsal and lateral stripes; the dorsal stripe fades near the end of the abdomen. Host plants pines.

A

B 1

B 2

A   Juniper Hairstreak   *Callophrys gryneus gryneus*

Underside, Logan County

Wingspan up to 1¼ inches. Only green hairstreak. Upperside is dull orange with brown margin. Underside bright to olive green: white spots on forewing in an even line, jagged on the hindwing, with two white basal spots and orange eye-spot. Habitat open areas near cedars. Breeding resident with two broods. Well camouflaged on cedar branches, easily flushed. Flight April–September. Common statewide.

Larva is deep green with oblique white bars on each segment and a broken white lateral stripe. Larvae eat tips of new foliage. Host plant Eastern Redcedar.

B   Oak Hairstreak   *Satyrium favonius ontario*

Underside, Poinsett County

Wingspan up to 1½ inches. Aka Southern Hairstreak. Underside grayish brown: narrow orangish red cap on blue tail-spot, hindwing with white-edged inner black line forming a "W." Forewing has nearly straight inner white line. Habitat woodlands, forests, and scrub. Breeding resident with one brood. Flight May–June. Uncommon statewide.

Larva is variable: green or pink, covered with tiny pale spots. Host plants members of the oak family.

The similar **Hickory Hairstreak,** *Satyrium caryaevorum*, has a wingspan up to 1⅜ inches. Underside dark gray with band of white-edged dashes on both sides. Blue tail-spot extends inward, touching inner band. Habitat deciduous woods and forest clearings. Breeding resident with one brood. Flight May–July. Rare, inhabits the Ozarks, and is a species of special concern. Easily confused with the other banded hairstreaks. Larva is yellow-green with a dark dorsal stripe and distinct diagonal stripes along the sides. Host plants Bitternut and other hickories.

Edward's Hairstreak, *Satyrium edwardsii,* has a wingspan up to 1⅜ inches. Underside is brownish gray, with two red crescents above blue tail-spot, and a band of uneven separate dark spots encircled with white. Habitat woodlands and barrens with scrub oaks. Breeding resident with one brood. Flight May–July. Rare to uncommon, known from the northern half of state. Larva reddish brown, darker dorsally, with whitish lateral dashes. Host plant scrub oak.

A

B

A   Coral Hairstreak   *Satyrium titus*
Underside, Lawrence County

Wingspan up to 1½ inches. Tailless, no eyespot. Underside brownish gray with band of coral-red spots along margin, and black spots encircled with white near the middle. Habitat open areas such as old fields and woodland edges. Almost always seen on Butterfly Milkweed. Breeding resident with one brood. Flight May–September. Uncommon to locally common. Nearly statewide except southeast Coastal Plain and Delta.

Larva yellow-green or green with pink patches on each end and over thorax and feeds at night. Host plants Black Cherry and Wild Plum.

B   Banded Hairstreak   *Satyrium calanus*
Underside, Logan County

Wingspan up to 1⅜ inches. Underside dark gray with band of white-edged dashes, usually just on outer edge. Blue tail-spot does not touch inner band. Habitat oak-hickory forest edges, glades. Breeding resident with one brood. Flight May–July. Uncommon to common statewide.

Larva variable in color, with dark patches on thorax and rear end; body usually has oblique lines. Host plants hickories and oaks.

C   King's Hairstreak   *Satyrium kingi*
Underside, Logan County

Wingspan up to 1⅜ inches. Underside brown with band of white-edged dashes; two dashes, nearly equal, form a broken "V" near the outer angle. Blue tail-spot has distinct red-orange cap. Habitat moist woodlands. Breeding resident with one brood. Flight May–July. Local and rare, a species of special concern. Known mainly from central and south Arkansas.

Larva is green with light oblique stripes. Host plant common sweetleaf.

The **Striped Hairstreak,** *Satyrium liparops,* has a wingspan up to 1⅜ inches. Underside brownish gray with numerous white stripes, distinguishing it from other striped hairstreaks. Blue tail-spot has a red-orange cap. Habitat forest edges and wetlands. Breeding resident with one brood. Flight May–June. Rare to uncommon statewide. Larva is emerald green with faint oblique lines. Host plants numerous including Black Cherry, Wild Plum, blueberry, and oaks.

A

B

C

A   Red-banded Hairstreak   *Calycopis cecrops*

Underside, Chicot County

Wingspan up to 1⅛ inches. Upperside black with some blue. Underside grayish brown. White lines are inwardly edged with a broad red band. Blue tail-spot with thin or no red cap. Habitat open areas including woodlands, fields, forest edges. This hairstreak feeds on flower nectar, but spends most of its time near the ground. Breeding resident with several broods. Flight April–October. Common statewide.

Larva is gray to brown and covered with short hairs (setae) and develops slowly. Host plants fallen leaves of sumacs, wax myrtle, and oaks.

B   White M Hairstreak   *Parrhasius m-album*

Underside, Craighead County

Wingspan up to 1½ inches. Upperside black with iridescent blue, but rarely seen. Underside grayish brown; hindwing has a white, black-edged line forming an "M" (or a "W") near the anal angle. Look for a white spot on the costa near the base of the hindwing, and a large red spot above the blue tail-spot. Habitat woodlands and forests. Breeding resident with several broods. Flight March–October. Rare statewide.

Larva is variable: green to yellowish green or red, covered with tiny white dots and pale oblique lines. Rust-colored dorsal spots may or may not be present. Host plants members of the oak family.

C   Gray Hairstreak   *Strymon melinus*

1) Underside, Logan County
2) Larva, Logan County

Wingspan up to 1¼ inches. This is the most common and widespread hairstreak in Arkansas. Abdomen orange on males, gray on females. Upperside dark gray with orange eyespot near tail. Underside gray with broken white and black lines, inwardly edged with orange; hindwing has orange tail-spots. Habitat most open areas such as gardens, woodland edges, roadsides, and other disturbed areas. Breeding resident with several broods. Flight March–November. Common statewide.

Larva is variable: green, pink, red, or brown with oblique lines and setae. Host plants flowers and fruits of numerous plants including lantana, legumes, corn, and cotton.

A

B

C 1

C 2

A   Eastern Tailed-Blue   *Cupido comyntas*
1) Upperside ♀, Logan County
2) Underside, Franklin County

Wingspan up to 1 inch. The only blue with tails. Upperside ♂ iridescent blue, ♀ brownish gray, with some blue in spring; both sexes have a few orange spots near tail. Underside light gray with black spots, with two orange spots near tail. Habitat open areas, especially disturbed areas. Males often seen mud-puddling in large groups. Breeding resident with several broods. Flight April–November. Common statewide.

Larva is variable: green to red, with dorsal and lateral stripes, covered with long setae and tiny white star-shaped setae. Host plants are flowers and seeds of many legumes.

B   Spring Azure   *Celastrina ladon*
Underside, Hot Spring County

Wingspan up to 1⅜ inches. Variable. Celastrina species make up the "Spring Azure Complex." Upperside ♂ blue, ♀ blue with black on forewing along apex and outer wing margin. Underside light gray with small black spots. Habitat deciduous woodland and forest edges, gardens. Breeding resident with one brood. Flight March–May. Common statewide.

Larva is variable in color and pattern: usually green, with or without marks and tiny white star-shaped setae. Host plants are flowers of several trees and wild-flowers including dogwood, viburnum, Black Cherry, and New Jersey tea.

The **Summer Azure,** *Celastrina neglecta,* is similar in almost every aspect to the Spring Azure, but adults are whiter. Breeding resident with several broods. Flight late May–October. Common statewide.

Dusky Azure, *Celastrina nigra,* has a wingspan up to 1¼ inches. Upperside ♂ grayish black; ♀ has some light blue. Underside with a row of black crescents and dots along outer margins. Habitat shady deciduous woods and disturbed areas. Breeding resident with one brood. Flight April–May. Local and rare, recorded from Washington and Nevada Counties. Larva green, host plant Goatsbeard.

The **Appalachian Azure,** *Celastrina neglectamajor*, has a wingspan up to 1½ inches. Underside chalk white. Habitat rich, deciduous and mixed woods. Colonist in low numbers with one brood. Flight May–June. Rare in the Ozarks. Larva is as variable as larvae of other azures. Host plant Black Cohosh, aka Black Snakeroot.

A 1

A 2

B

A   Silvery Blue   *Glaucopsyche lygdamus lygdamus*
Underside, Hot Spring County

Wingspan up to 1¼ inches. Upperside ♂ iridescent blue, ♀ dark with some blue; both have black margin with white fringe. Underside gray with a row of round black spots encircled with white. Habitat open areas near woods. Breeding resident with one brood. Flight March–May. Locally rare to common. Inhabits the western part of the state, mainly the Ouachita Mountains. It can be easily confused with other blues.

Larva is green to pink with green or pink dorsal stripe and chevrons and short setae. Like so many other caterpillars in this family, Silvery Blues are tended by ants. Host plants flowers and seeds of vetches and lupines.

B   Reakirt's Blue   *Echinargus isola*
Underside, Logan County

Wingspan up to 1⅛ inches. Upperside ♂ purplish blue, ♀ grayish brown with some blue basally. Underside gray: forewing has a band of distinct round black spots encircled with white; hindwing has black spots near anal angle and grayish white crescents along outer margin. Habitat open areas, such as fields, pastures, woodlands, and forest edges. Breeding resident with several broods. Flight April–October. Uncommon; nearly statewide except for the southeastern part of the Delta.

Larva variable: green, yellow-green, or red with dorsal chevrons. Host plants buds and flowers of legumes.

Additional Coppers, Hairstreaks, and Blues That Occasionally Stray into Arkansas:

C   Marine Blue   *Leptotes marina*
Underside, Criaghead County.

Wingspan up to 1⅛ inches. This striking, zebra-stripe-patterned butterfly wanders into Arkansas almost every year in low numbers.

Cassius Blue, *Leptotes cassius*
Western Pygmy Blue, *Brephidium exilis*

A

B

C

Metalmarks (Family Riodinidae)

Our metalmarks are small brown-and-orange butterflies named for the metallic markings on their wings above and below. Some authorities recognize metalmarks as a subfamily in the Lycaenidae. The front pair of male legs is reduced. Their eyes are green, and the antennae are striped. Adults perch with their wings spread open, often underneath the surface of a leaf, and drink flower nectar. The two metalmark species in Arkansas look very similar and are difficult to separate in the field, so habitat may be the only reliable way to separate them. Metalmarks overwinter as partially grown larvae.

These are species of special concern. Much habitat has been lost through development, host plants being crowded out by invasive species, or perhaps pesticide use. The good news is there has been an increase in wetlands awareness and protection, and the Swamp Metalmark may benefit from a recovery plan.

A   Northern Metalmark   *Calephelis borealis*

Upperside, Faulkner County

Wingspan up to 1¼ inches. Upperside dark reddish brown with silvery blue bands, darker in the middle with pattern of black lines. Underside bright orange. Habitat openings in limestone and shale woodlands. Breeding resident with one or two broods. Flight May–June, August. Locally rare to locally uncommon. Colonies scattered throughout the Interior Highlands.

Larva is whitish gray with rows of long hairs. Host plant Roundleaf Ragwort.

B   Swamp Metalmark   *Calephelis muticum*

Upperside, Washington County

Wingspan up to ⅞ inch. Upperside orange-brown with silvery blue bands, pattern of black lines in the middle. Underside bright orange. Habitat wetlands. Breeding resident with one or two broods. Flight June, August. Local, rare, widely distributed throughout the Ozarks. Recorded from Washington, Carroll, Marion, and Independence Counties.

Larva is yellowish brown with rows of long hairs. Host plants Swamp Thistle, recorded in three places in the Ouachita Mountains, and Tall Thistle, which is found nearly statewide.

A

B

The wild bee and the butterfly
Are bright and happy things to see,
Living beneath a summer sky.

—*Eliza Cook*

Brushfoots (Family Nymphalidae)

This is the largest family of butterflies, called brushfoots because the first pair of legs is reduced and covered with short hairs like a little brush and is used to clean the mouthparts. Many of our most beloved large butterflies are in this family, such as the Diana Fritillary, Mourning Cloak, Red-spotted Purple, and Viceroy. The adults vary in size and color, and this family has the strongest migrants like the Monarch and Painted Lady.

Many adults have developed methods of evading predators such as warning colors to signal toxicity, mimicry of toxic butterflies, camouflage, and eyespots. Adults also vary in their choice of nutritional resources. Many feed on flower nectar, but some adults take liquids from animal droppings, rotting fruit, and from animal carcasses. This family includes the longest-living adults, such as the Mourning Cloak and Monarch.

Larvae are just as diverse as adults, smooth to spiny, some solitary, some feeding communally. The chrysalises are suspended by the cremaster. Brushfoots overwinter as larvae or adults.

Gulf Fritillary (upperside)

Monarch   *Danaus plexippus*

1) Upperside ♂, Logan County
2) Upperside ♀, Logan County
3) Larva, Logan County
4) Tagged Monarch, Logan County

Wingspan up to 4½ inches. Wings are an eye-catching cinnamon orange with black veins and white dots on black wing borders. The male wing veins have thin pigmentation, the females have thick pigmentation, and males have swollen pouches in the middle of the hindwings. Habitat most open areas, including urban settings. Late spring and summer breeding resident with one or two broods. Flight March–November. Uncommon to common statewide, and seen mainly during fall migration.

The larva is a master of warning coloration with yellow, black, and white cross bands and long black filaments at both ends. This large, smooth caterpillar is safe for children to pet, and is great for classrooms because the life cycle takes about thirty days. Host plants young milkweed leaves, especially Tropical and Butterfly Milkweed. Milkweed contains toxic compounds called cardenolides, and the larva builds up a concentration that extends to the adult. The chrysalis becomes transparent just before the adult emerges.

Monarchs are famous for their annual migration to their sanctuaries in central Mexico, and this biological phenomenon is not completely understood. When early fall Monarchs emerge, they are different from earlier generations. Shorter days and cooler temperatures in the North are triggers. These Monarchs can live up to nine months because they are fairly inactive once they reach their winter sanctuaries, surviving on stored fat. The summer adults live only a few weeks. The monarchs that make the journey south don't mate or lay eggs until they fly north in the spring. Their thick wings are adapted for the long flight. The journey north begins in early spring, with Monarchs arriving in Arkansas late March and April, and females laying eggs on whatever milkweed they can find. The life cycle completes in a month, and the "children" of the migrants continue north. This cycle repeats until the butterflies reach the northern part of the country, and then the "great-great-grand-children" of the migrants begin the journey south, to a place they have never been before, but somehow each year's migrants know where to go.

Sometimes Monarchs breed in Arkansas in late summer if young milkweed leaves are available, so cut back spent blooms and branching plants to encourage new leaf growth and new blooms.

Thousands of Monarchs are "tagged" by citizens each year through a program directed by Monarch Watch. Tagging Monarchs is a way to gather data that helps scientists understand the mysteries of migration. Information on Monarch Watch is listed in the Resources section.

1

2

3

4

A   Gulf Fritillary   *Agraulis vanillae*

1) Underside, Logan County
2) Larva, Craighead County

Wingspan up to 3 inches. There is no mistaking this butterfly for any other; it's one of our "ooh" butterflies, and just a thrill to see. Forewings elongated. Upperside bright orange with black marks; forewing has three white spots encircled with black. Underside brownish with elongated silver spots. Habitat a variety of open areas, including urban settings. Summer breeding resident; life cycle is about one month, so there may be several broods throughout the summer into fall as long as the host plant is available and weather permits. Migrants usually begin appearing late spring and fly as long as weather allows. Uncommon to common statewide with migrants in sporadic numbers each year.

Larva is shiny, orange with black or purple stripes and long black spines. Host plant passion-vine.

B   Variegated Fritillary   *Euptoieta claudia*

1) Upperside, Logan County
2) Larva, Logan County

Wingspan up to 2½ inches. Upperside orange-brown with black lines and a row of black spots along the wing margin. Underside brown mottled with orange and cream. The forewing cell has a distinct orange spot encircled with black. Habitat a variety of open areas. Summer breeding resident, may have several broods if conditions are favorable. Migrants usually begin appearing mid-spring and fly as long as weather allows. Uncommon to common statewide with migrants in sporadic numbers each year.

Larva is shiny, reddish orange, with black-edged white stripes and rows of black spines. Two spines on the head point forward and have clubbed tips. Larvae graze from plant to plant, often seen moving on the ground off the host. Host plants numerous including passion-vine, violets, and flax.

A 1

A 2

B 1

B 2

Diana Fritillary   *Speyeria diana*

1) Upperside ♂, Logan County
2) Upperside ♀, Logan County
3) Underside ♀ and ♂, Logan County
4) Larva, Logan County

Wingspan up to 4½ inches. Also known simply as "Diana," this is Arkansas's "showcase butterfly" and one of the best examples of sexual dimorphism. Upperside ♂ dark brown at base, broad orange outer margin. Underside orange and rather plain. Upperside ♀ black with blue on outer hindwing margin, rows of white spots on forewing. Underside dark brownish blue and rather plain. Females mimic the distasteful Pipevine Swallowtail. Males emerge a few weeks before females, and wander widely.

Dianas require high-quality nectar sources such as Butterfly Milkweed, Purple Coneflower, ironweed, Bee Balm, and coreopsis. They readily visit domesticated flowers such as pentas, lantana, and butterfly bush. These butterflies are relatively long-lived, surviving several months. Habitat open moist (mesic) forests, prairies, and wetlands. Breeding resident with one brood. Flight mid May to early October. From May to July, males are seen more often than females, and emerge two to three weeks before females. Adults may estivate through August. Mostly females reemerge to fly September to early October; most males have died. Uncommon to locally common in colonies scattered throughout the Interior Highlands and northern Coastal Plain. Although this butterfly is not as imperiled as once thought, it is still a species of concern because its population dynamics are not well understood. This species may have been overlooked in the past, and forest management regimes are benefiting the butterflies with an increase in their nectar sources. There are some "Hot Spots" in Arkansas in June where it is common to see several males nectaring on a stand of Butterfly Milkweed with lots of other butterflies. Solitary females are seen more often late morning to early evening.

Larva is blackish purple with black branching spines. The lower third of the spines are reddish orange. The top of head is angular, almost horned, and orange; the rest of the head is black. Females lay eggs in the vicinity of host plants. Fritillary eggs take several weeks to develop. The first instar overwinters. Larvae are elusive and feed nocturnally. Eggs and first instar larvae may perish due to fungus and disease as well as freezing temperatures. Host plants violets.

1

2

3

4

Great Spangled Fritillary   *Speyeria cybele cybele*

1) Upperside, Logan County
2) Underside, Logan County
3) Larva, Carroll County
4) With Diana ♂

Wingspan up to 4 inches. Upperside orange with black markings, darker at the base. Underside rich orange-brown; forewing has black markings, hindwing has rows of silver spots. Habitat open woodlands and forests, meadows, and disturbed areas with high-quality nectar sources. Breeding resident with one brood. Flight mid May to early October. Males emerge a few weeks before females, life history similar to Diana. Common statewide except from southern Coastal Plain and Delta.

Larva is black with black branching spines. The lower half of the spines are orange. Head is orange above and black below. These are very subtle differences from the Diana larva. Females lay eggs in the vicinity of host plants. The first instar overwinters without eating. Larvae are elusive and feed nocturnally. Host plants violets.

One of the thrills of summer is the sight of twenty or more Great Spangled Fritillaries on a stand of Butterfly Milkweed. The Great Spangled Fritillary is often mistaken for the male Diana, so a comparison photo is provided as an aid.

1

2

3

4

A   Gorgone Checkerspot   *Chlosyne gorgone*

1) Upperside, Logan County
2) Underside, Logan County

Wingspan up to 1¼ inches. Upperside orange with bold marks, checkered fringe; hindwing black border has pale orange chevrons. Underside brownish orange with distinctive pattern of white zigzags and black spots. Habitat forest edges and other open areas. Breeding resident with several broods. Flight April–July. Local and rare, known from central and western counties.

Larva variable: black or orange with light lateral stripes, black head, and spines. Host plants members of the aster family.

B   Silvery Checkerspot   *Chlosyne nycteis*

Upperside, Logan County

Wingspan up to 2 inches. Upperside orange, heavily marked with black borders, patches, and spots, some with white centers. Underside hindwing has white median band and incomplete band of white crescents along outer margin. Habitat forest edges, gardens, and other open areas. Breeding resident with several broods. Flight April–September. Common statewide.

Larva is black with black spines, may or may not have orange lateral stripe. The spines are brown in the orange stripe. Head black and shiny. Larvae feed communally until the third instar. Host plants asters, Black-eyed Susan, and sunflowers.

C   Phaon Crescent   *Phyciodes phaon*

Upperside, Mississippi County

Wingspan up to 1½ inches. Upperside forewing orange and black; forewing has cream median band. Underside tan with black lines, forewing with orange area (disc), hindwing with a pale crescent within black area. Habitat open, moist areas where host plant occurs. Breeding resident with two broods. Flight May–October. Locally common in the northeast, uncommon elsewhere.

Larva is brown with black dorsal and lateral stripes. Host plant Fog Fruit (*Phyla*).

A 1

A 2

B

C

A   Pearl Crescent   *Phyciodes tharos*

Upperside, Logan County

Wingspan up to 1½ inches. One of our most common butterflies. Upperside
orange with black bars, lines, and spots; hindwings have orange crescents along
outer margin. Underside hindwing yellowish orange with brown lines, and a
pale crescent surrounded by a brown patch. Habitat nearly all open areas.
Breeding resident with several broods. Flight April–November. Common
statewide.

Larva is dark brown with brown spines and white dots. Shiny black head with
white lines. Host plants asters.

B   Baltimore Checkerspot   *Euphydryas phaeton ozarkae*

1) Upperside, Washington County
2) Underside, Washington County

Wingspan up to 2¾ inches. This butterfly is very unique with a distinctive bold
pattern and colors. Upperside black with white spots on the outer half of wings;
outer margin is lined with orange crescents. Underside dazzling array of alternating orange and white spots separated by black. Habitat wet meadows and dry
fields, floodplains. Breeding resident with one brood. Flight June–July. Local,
rare to uncommon in scattered colonies throughout the Ozarks. This rare butterfly is of special concern.

Larva has orange and black cross bands, black head and rear, and black branched
spines. Larvae feed together, overwinter from August until spring. Host plant
Turtlehead before overwintering. Spring host plants plantain, viburnum, honey-
suckle, and Lousewort.

A

B 1

B 2

Common Buckeye   *Junonia coenia*

1) Upperside, Logan County
2) Larva, Franklin County

Wingspan up to 2½ inches. Upperside brown, forewing with a white bar that partially surrounds the large eyespot, and two orange bars in the cell. Hindwing has a large and small eyespot with an orange band. Underside seasonally variable: tan or brown (summer form), or rose red (form "rosa," winter or short-day) due to cold temperatures or short photoperiod. Males establish territories and perch to find mates. A male will investigate anything entering his territory and chase away other males. Habitat nearly all open areas. Summer breeding resident with several broods. Flight April–December. Common statewide, especially during fall migration.

Larva is black and white dorsally, with white lateral stripes. Spines are blue-black dorsally, black with orange base laterally. Orange head with two short black spines on top. Host plants numerous, including snapdragon, toadflax, false foxglove, plaintain, Gerardia, and ruellia.

1

2

A   Question Mark   *Polygonia interrogationis*

1) Underside, Logan County
2) Larva, Craighead County

Wingspan up to 2½ inches. Angled wings. Seasonally variable. Upperside orange with black spots, hindwings orange with violet wing margins (winter) or mostly black (summer). Underside brown, looks just like a leaf, hindwing with a central white question mark shape. This mark looks much like the question mark used in punctuation, but sometimes the imagination must be used. Underside of winter form is mostly brown, of summer form mottled brown and black. Adults occasionally feed on flower nectar; primarily adult resources are tree sap, fruit juice, and scat. Habitat woodlands, forests, and urban areas. Breeding resident with two broods. Flight year round during mild winters; the second brood adult overwinters. Common statewide, migratory.

Larva is variable: gray, black, or yellow, with orange or cream stripes and orange spines. Host plants elms, hackberries, nettles, and hops.

B   Eastern Comma   *Polygonia comma*

Underside, Randolph County

Wingspan up to 2 inches. Seasonally variable. Angled wings. Upperside forewing orange with black spots, hindwing black (summer) or orange with black dots (winter). Underside mottled black and brown, looks like a leaf; hindwing has a central white comma marking that looks very similar to the punctuation mark, except both ends are swollen. Habitat open woodlands and forests. Breeding resident with two broods. Flight February–December, year round during mild winters. Common statewide.

Larva is variable: green, black, yellow, or cream with yellow or white spines and red dots above spiracles. Host plants nettles, elms, and hops.

The **Gray Comma,** *Polygonia progne,* has a wingspan up to 2¼ inches. Upperside forewing orange with black spots, hindwing outer half black with orange dots. Underside has thin barklike brown and gray lines, and thin silver "comma" mark. Habitat woodlands and forests. Breeding resident with two broods. Flight July–October. Local, rare to uncommon in the Ozarks. Larva brown with black lateral dashes and yellow spines. Host plant gooseberry.

A 1

A 2

B

A   Mourning Cloak   *Nymphalis antiopa*

1) Upperside, Logan County
2) Larva, Logan County

Wingspan up to 3½ inches. This butterfly has it all: long life and beauty. It produces an audible "click" when disturbed, all you see is a flash of the colorful
upperside, and it disappears. This butterfly can bring people out of a winter
funk. Wings have a parchmentlike texture and irregular shape. Upperside deep
purplish brown with a row of iridescent blue spots along outer margin and
bright yellow border. Underside resembles tree bark; blackish brown with dark
fine lines and cream border. The adults may live ten to eleven months. These butterflies sip tree sap and fruit juice instead of flower nectar. Habitat woodlands,
forests, glades, and urban areas with trees. Breeding resident with one brood.
Flight nearly year round; adults overwinter and emerge on warm winter days.
Common statewide in small numbers. Adults usually emerge in summer, estivate until fall, seek out a shelter, overwinter until March or April, fly again, and
breed.

Larva is black, covered with small white dots, eight reddish orange dorsal spots,
and branching black spines. Larvae feed together and can defoliate branches.
Host plants willows, elms, hackberry, cottonwood, and others.

B   Red Admiral   *Vanessa atalanta*

1) Upperside, Logan County
2) Larva, Craighead County

Wingspan up to 2½ inches. Upperside brownish black with bright orange bands;
forewing band is darker, with white spots on outer part near apex. Underside
forewing reddish orange, blue, and white, hindwing mottled black and brown,
much like a leaf. Males establish territories and perch to find mates. A male will
investigate anything entering his territory and chase away other males. Adults are
seldom seen on flowers, preferring tree sap and fermenting fruit. Habitat forest
edges, gardens, and other open areas. Breeding resident with two broods. Adults
overwinter as pupae or adults, and are migratory. Flight March–November;
adults may be seen flying on warm winter days. Common statewide.

Larva is variable: may be white, yellowish-green, or black, covered with white
specks, uneven lateral cream stripe on abdominal segments, spines yellow or
black. Black head has whitish hairs and spines. Larvae build nests by rolling
and/or tying leaves of the host plant; older caterpillars may use a single folded
leaf. Host plants nettles and False Nettle.

A 1

A 2

B 1

B 2

A   Painted Lady *Vanessa cardui*
  1) Underside, Logan County
  2) Larva, Logan County

Wingspan up to 2½ inches. Upperside pinkish orange with black margins and bars. Forewing has distinctive marks: white spots near apex, black bar complete in the middle. Hindwing margin has a row of small black spots and a blue dash. Underside forewing colored with orange-pink, hindwing mottled white and brown, with four small eyespots, a faint fifth on top. Habitat nearly all open areas, anywhere flowers occur. Breeding resident with two broods. Flight March–November. Adult overwinters and is a strong migrant. Common statewide.

Larva is variable: usually brown with yellow stripes and dashes, yellow or gray spines and hair. Larva makes a silk nest with leaves. Host plants numerous including thistle and other members of the aster family, hollyhock, and lupine.

B   American Lady *Vanessa virginiensis*
  1) Underside, Logan County
  2) Larva, Logan County

Wingspan up to 2⅛ inches. Aka Virginia Lady. Upperside orange with dark brown margins and bars. Forewing has a few distinctive marks: white spots near apex, black bar broken in the middle, and a tiny white dot in the orange on the outer margin. Hindwing margin has a row of small blue spots. Underside has ornate color and streak pattern with two large eyespots. Habitat nearly all open areas, anywhere flowers occur. Breeding resident with several broods. Flight March–November, seen most often late summer through fall. Adults overwinter and are migratory. Common statewide.

Larva is variable: usually black with yellow cross bands, seven white dorsal spots, and branched spines with red bases. Larva makes a silk nest with leaves. Host plants Pearly Everlasting, Pussytoes, and other members of the aster family.

A 1

A 2

B 1

B 2

Red-spotted Purple   *Limenitis arthemis astyanax*

1) Upperside, Logan County
2) Underside, Craighead County
3) Larva, Logan County
4) ♀ Diana Fritillary (for comparison)

Wingspan up to 3¾ inches. Wings black with iridescent blue, dazzling in bright sunlight. Upperside forewing has a few red spots near wing apex, hindwing almost completely iridescent blue-green. Underside has reddish orange spots near wing bases and along outer margins. Habitat woodland and forest edges. Adults visit mud, carnivore scat, rotting fruit, and sap, but they do visit flowers. Males perch on trees in open areas to search for females. Breeding resident with two broods. Flight March–October. Common statewide.

Larva looks like a bird dropping with attitude: brownish black or green with a white saddle. Larva has a humped thorax with two branched horns. The larva overwinters inside a winter nest made of a rolled leaf and silk called a hibernaculum. Host plants numerous, including Black Cherry, willows, and oaks.

The Red-spotted Purple is a mimic of the distasteful Pipevine Swallowtail, as is the Diana Fritillary. The Red-spotted Purple is often mistaken for the female Diana Fritillary. Looking at the photograph, notice the Red-spotted Purple does not have nearly the same blue and white pattern of the Diana, and, of course, the undersides are completely different, if you turn back to look at the Diana photos. Red-spotted Purples often gather at mud or streamside in large groups; female Dianas do not. With a little practice, you will notice most individual Red-spotted Purples are much smaller than female Dianas. The presence of both butterflies is a sign of quality habitat.

1

2

3

4

A   Viceroy   *Limenitis archippus archippus*

1) Upperside, Pope County
2) Larva, Pope County

Wingspan up to 3 inches. Wings orange with black veins on both sides, with white spots near the forewing apex. The mark to look for is the black line that bisects the hindwing on both sides. Habitat open wet areas such as ponds, lakes, and streams. Breeding resident with two broods. Flight April–October. Uncommon statewide. This butterfly is famous for mimicking the Monarch, but new research suggests it is also distasteful. Refer to pp. 10–11 for photos of the two together and mimicry description.

Larva looks like a bird dropping, very similar to the closely related Red-spotted Purple; usually green but may be brown, with a white saddle and a humped thorax with two branched horns. Larva overwinters in a hibernaculum. Host plants members of the willow family.

B   Goatweed Leafwing   *Anaea andria*

1) Underside, Logan County
2) Larva, Craighead County

Wingspan up to 3 inches. Seasonal and sexually dimorphic, all mimic dead leaves. Upperside generally reddish orange; ♀ has orange-brown wing margins. Underside brown with some gray. Adults don't sit still very long, and are attracted to mud, rotting fruit, tree sap, and animal waste. Habitat open woodlands and forests. Breeding resident with two broods. Flight February–December. Adults overwinter and fly on warm winter days. Common statewide.

Larva is green to grayish green, with small raised white bumps. Host plant goatweed (*Croton*).

A 1

A 2

B 1

B 2

A   Hackberry Emperor   *Asterocampa celtis celtis*

1) Upperside, Logan County
2) Larva, Craighead County

Wingspan up to 2¼ inches. Upperside brown, white, and black. Forewing has one big eyespot, a row of white spots, and a black bar with two black spots in the cell near costa. Hindwing has a row of black spots. Underside gray with eyespots and brown lines. Habitat hackberry woods. Adults perch on trees, feed on sap and rotting fruit. Breeding resident with two broods. Flight May–October. Common statewide.

Larva is green with two "antlers" on head, and forked "tails." Yellow spots and stripes extend from the antlers down the body, covered with tiny white dots. Half-grown caterpillars turn brown and overwinter together in curled host plant leaves. Host plant hackberry.

B   Tawny Emperor   *Asterocampa clyton clyton*

Upperside, Clay County

Wingspan up to 2¼ inches. Upperside orangish brown with two black bars in cell. Hindwing has a row of black spots. Underside brownish gray with black lines and faint eyespots on hindwing. Habitat hackberry woods. Adults feed on sap and rotting fruit. Breeding resident with two broods. Flight May–September. Uncommon statewide.

Larva similar to Hackberry Emperor, but with more stripes and longer antlers. Larvae feed communally through the third instar, then are solitary. They overwinter together in curled leaves. Host plant hackberry.

C   American Snout   *Libytheana carinenta*

Underside, Logan County

Wingspan up to 2 inches. Labial palps, known as the "snout," are long. The forewing tips are squared off. Upperside brown; forewing has white spots, orange at base. Underside gray with violet tinge, looks like a dead leaf. Habitat riparian areas, woodland edges, and lakesides. Breeding resident with two broods. Flight February–December, may be seen on warm winter days. Common statewide; migrants increase numbers.

Larva is yellowish green with yellow or white dorsal and lateral stripes and covered with rows of small white spots. The larva has the interesting habit of resting with the thorax arched. Adults overwinter. Host plant hackberry.

A 1

A 2

B

C

A   Northern Pearly-Eye   *Enodia anthedon*

Underside, Newton County

Wingspan up to 2½ inches. Upperside brown with outer band of black spots
encircled with yellow. Underside brownish gray with dark brown lines and eyespots, the forewing eyespots in a straight line. Habitat woodlands and forests,
usually with a nearby stream or spring. Breeding resident with two broods.
Flight May–September. Uncommon to locally common statewide.

Larva is smooth, greenish yellow or brown with forked "tails" and short reddish
horns on head. Larvae feed at night and overwinter. Host plants bottlebrush
grass, broadleaf uniola, white grass, and other grasses.

The **Southern Pearly-Eye,** *Enodia portlandia missarkae,* has a wingspan up to 2¼
inches. It differs from the Northern Pearly-Eye, having more white on the
underside and curved forewing eyespots. Habitat canebrakes in mesic woods.
Breeding resident with several broods. Flight May–September. Local; rare
statewide even in the right habitat. Larva similar to Northern Pearly-Eye. Host
plants giant cane and switch cane.

B   Creole Pearly-Eye   *Enodia creola*

Underside, Craighead County

Wingspan up to 2¼ inches. Upperside similar to other Pearly-Eyes. Underside
with dark brown lines, forewing with straight row of eyespots, dark brown
median band bending outward. Habitat canebrakes in deep woods. Breeding resident with two broods. Flight May–September. Local, rare statewide, even in the
right habitat.

Larva similar to Northern Pearly-Eye. Host plant switch cane.

C   Gemmed Satyr   *Cyllopsis gemma*

Underside, Cross County

Wingspan up to 1½ inches. Upperside light brown, seldom seen. Underside light
brown with silver-gray patch on hindwing margin with four metallic black spots.
Habitat open grassy woodlands, where it perches close to the ground. Breeding
resident with several broods. Flight April–October. Common statewide.

Larva green with yellow stripes; head has red-tipped horns. Host plants
Bermuda grass and other grasses.

A

B

C

A   Carolina Satyr   *Hermeuptychia sosybius*
Underside, Logan County

Wingspan up to 1½ inches. Upperside plain brown. Underside wings have dark brown lines and outer margin of eyespots, one black with white center on forewing, three on hindwing. Habitat woodlands and forests. Breeding resident with several broods. Flight April–October. Common statewide.

Larva is green, covered with short white hairs. Short forked tail, no horns on head. Host plants grasses.

The **Georgia Satyr,** *Neonympha areolatus,* has a wingspan up to 2 inches. Upperside plain brown. Underside brown with orange bands, hindwing with elongate metallic silver eyespots encircled with yellow, eyespots surrounded with orange. Habitat sandy pinewoods or barrens. Breeding resident with two broods. Flight May–September. Local, rare, recorded from the southern edge of the state, not well known. Larva yellow-green with yellow stripes, head green with tan bumps. Host plants sedges.

B   Little Wood-Satyr   *Megisto cymela*
Underside, Logan County

Wingspan up to 1¾ inches. Wings brown with two black eyespots encircled with yellow on both sides and dark brown lines. Underside hindwing has two extra yellow-rimmed silver spots next to eyespots. Habitat open woodlands and forests. Breeding resident with several broods. Flight April–August. Common statewide, mostly in summer.

Larva is light brown with white stripes, dark lateral dashes, and short spines, and active at night. Host plants grasses.

C   Common Wood-Nymph   *Cercyonis pegala pegala*
Underside, Logan County

Wingspan up to 3 inches. Variable. Wings dark brown; forewing has large yellow patch with two eyespots, hindwing has small eyespots. Underside heavily marked with fine brownish black lines. Habitat open grassy areas and forest edges. Breeding resident with one brood. Males may live only two to three weeks; females may live a few months. Egg-laying occurs in late summer to early fall, much like fritillaries. Flight June–October. Common statewide.

Larva is green or greenish yellow with pale lateral stripes, and is covered with short hairs. Pink-tipped "tails." Host plants purple top and other grasses.

A

B

C

Additional Brushfoots That Occasionally Stray into and/or Form Temporary Colonies in Arkansas:

Queen, *Danaus gilippus*
Julia, *Dryas julia*
Zebra, *Heliconius charithonia*
Regal Fritillary, *Speyeria idalia,* is thought to have been extirpated from Arkansas since the late 1970s. This butterfly requires large tracts of high-quality prairie. It is most commonly seen in the Midwestern states of Kansas, Iowa, and Missouri. The Regal Fritillary is extremely vulnerable and is a conservation concern. Although not federally listed on the Endangered Species List, it should be considered endangered.
Texan Crescent, *Anthanassa texana*
Milbert's Tortoiseshell, *Aglais milberti*
Common Mestra, *Mestra amymone*
Appalachian Brown, *Satyrodes appalachia*

*Moth Descriptive
Text and Photographs*

Hurt no living thing:
Ladybird, nor butterfly,
Nor moth with dusty wing,
Nor cricket chirping cheerily
Nor grasshopper so light of leap,
Nor dancing gnat, nor beetle fat,
Nor harmless worms that creep.

—Christina Rossetti

Moth Upperside Wing Patterns

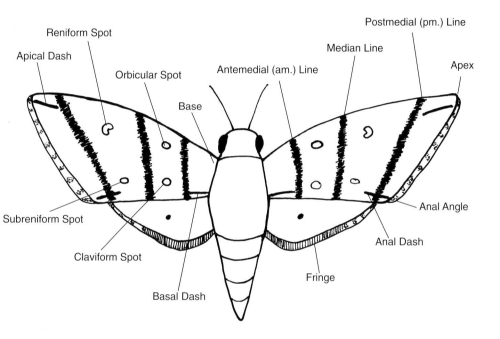

Yucca Moths (Family Prodoxidae)

This family of small moths is responsible for the pollination of specific flowers. Females have strong ovipositors, laying their eggs on the flower's stigma and simultaneously depositing pollen collected with specialized mouthparts best described as "tentacles." Larvae of this family bore into stems, seeds, or yucca fruits.

A   Yucca Moth   *Tegeticula yuccasella*

Upperside, Texas

Wingspan up to 1 inch. Forewings are white, no markings. Hindwing is grayish with white fringe. Habitat wherever yucca grows. Adults sometimes come to porch lights, but are often found within yucca flowers. Breeding resident with one brood. Flight early to midsummer when yucca blooms. Uncommon to common statewide.

Larva can be found inside the seed pods of yucca host plant, and pupate in the soil in spring.

Bagworm Moths (Family Psychidae)

This family of small moths is best known by the cases, or "bags," lived in by the larva and female. The females are legless and wingless. Some are serious pests of evergreens, especially ornamentals.

B   Bagworm Moth   *Thyridopteryx ephemeraeformis*

Larval case, Washington County

Wingspan up to 1 inch. Only males have wings, which are black but transparent. Body is black with tapered abdomen. Legless, wingless females remain in case and lay eggs. Habitat generally wherever evergreens grow. Breeding resident with one brood. Flight September–October. Common statewide wherever evergreens occur.

Larva dark; head is sometimes seen extending out of the bag to feed, and the larva can travel with this case, so it's quite the mobile home! Host plants evergreens and other trees and shrubs. The bag is covered with bits of the host plant, making it well camouflaged.

Cosmopterigid Moths (Family Cosmopterigidae)

The wings of these small moths are brightly colored, narrow, and pointed, with hindwings narrower than forewings.

A   *Euclemensia bassetellata*

Upperside, Logan County

Wingspan up to ⅝ inch. Body and wings shiny black; forewings have bright orange patches. Habitat forested areas. Attracted to lights. Breeding resident with several broods. Flight May–September. Common statewide.

Larva has a specific host: it parasitizes female gall-like scale insects in the *Kermes* genus.

Tropical Ermine Moths (Family Attevidae)

These small to medium moths have narrow, blunt wings and are colorful. The adults at rest are shaped like sticks. Larvae live together in webs spun around host plant leaves.

B   **Ailanthus Webworm Moth**   *Atteva punctella*

Upperside, Washington County

Wingspan up to 1¼ inches. Forewings orange, with four pale yellow spot bands circled with black. Hindwings, in contrast, are dark, smoky gray, and mostly transparent. Often seen at lights at night. Habitat variable, adults are often seen at lights. Breeding resident with several broods. Flight March–November. Common statewide.

Larva is brown. Host plant *Ailanthus*, which is an introduced tree that has escaped from urban areas and spread.

A

B

Clear-winged or Wasp Moths (Family Sesiidae)

Probably the easiest way to recognize these moths is by their resemblance to wasps, with mostly transparent or "clear" wings. The forewings are long and narrow and the hindwings broad. These moths are active during the day and seen on flowers. The larvae are pests, boring into roots, stems, canes, or trunks of the host plants.

A   Squash Vine Borer   *Melittia curcurbitae*
Upperside, Washington County

Wingspan up to 1¼ inches. The forewings are smoky black with a metallic sheen, the hindwings transparent. The orange abdomen and long, fuzzy orange and black hindwings are distinctive. Breeding resident with two broods. Flight April–November. Uncommon to common statewide wherever the host plants occur.

Larva bores into the stems of host plants, which are mainly squash, gourds, and pumpkins.

B   Riley's Clearwing   *Synanthedon rileyana*
Upperside, Washington County

Wingspan up to ⅞ inch. The forewings and hindwings are almost completely transparent, edged in black. There is a reddish orange bar near the outer edge of the forewings (reniform spot). The thorax and abdomen are black with yellow bands. Breeding resident with several broods. Flight May–September. Uncommon to common statewide.

Host plant Horse Nettle.

C   Peachtree Borer   *Synanthedon exitiosa*
Upperside ♀, Johnson County

Wingspan up to 1⅜ inches. Sexually dimorphic with ♀ forewings smoky black. Body blue-black with a broad reddish orange band; ♂ forewings clear; body has a yellow collar, bands, and streaks on thorax, abdomen, and legs. Breeding resident with one brood. Flight May–September. Common in orchards statewide.

Larva bores into the trunks of host plants, which are peach and other *Prunus*. Eggs are laid on lower tree trunks, and larvae usually bore into tree just below the ground surface, girdling the tree. Larvae overwinter in their burrows in the trees.

A

B

C

Carpenterworm Moths (Family Cossidae)

The largest members of the microlepidoptera, these moths are often mistaken for sphinx moths. But look at the antennae: ♀ threadlike, ♂ feathery. They do not feed as adults. Larvae can be serious timber pests.

A   Carpenterworm Moth   *Prionoxystus robiniae*

Upperside ♀, Logan County

Wingspan up to 3¼ inches. Sexually dimorphic: ♀ larger, wings mottled gray and black, somewhat transparent; ♂ forewing darker and less mottled, hindwing yellow and black. Both sexes well camouflaged. Habitat woodlands and forested areas. Breeding resident; the life cycle takes three to four years. Flight April–October. Uncommon statewide.

Larva, the Carpenterworm, is grublike and bores into trees. Host plants several hardwoods including ash, oaks, and willows.

Flannel Moths (Family Megalopygidae)

This is a small moth family. The moths and larvae are very hairy, hence the name "flannel." Be careful and respectful of the larvae because under all their hairs lurk poisonous, stinging spines. These caterpillars are best left alone because even the hairs may be irritating. Male antennae are feathery, female threadlike. Pupa overwinters in a cocoon on the host plant.

B   Crinkled Flannel Moth   *Megalopyge crispata*

Upperside, Washington County

Wingspan up to 1¼ inches. Also known as Black-waved Flannel Moth. Wings and body creamy yellow, very hairy. The forewing front edge (costa) has a few wavy black lines with a brown patch underneath. Habitat woodlands. Breeding resident with two broods. Flight May–October. Local, uncommon to common statewide.

Larva is covered with long hairs: white in first few instars, orange to gray later in development. The stinging spines underneath the hairs can pack a painful punch if touched. Host plants a variety of trees and shrubs including alders, apples, blackberry, Black Cherry, hackberry, oaks, Persimmon, Sassafras, and willows. Look for the larvae on the underside of young leaves; look for cocoons on lower tree trunks.

A

B

Window-winged Moths (Family Thyrididae)

These small to medium moths have stout bodies and transparent, windowlike spots in the wings. They are day fliers seen on flowers, and are often mistaken for butter-flies.

A   Mournful Thyris   *Thyris sepulchralis*

Upperside, Logan County

Wingspan up to 1 inch. Forewings black with white spots; the spots on the outer margin give the moth a torn appearance. There is a large white patch on the black hindwings. Habitat variable, found on flowers. Breeding resident with several broods. Flight April–August. Uncommon statewide.

Larva is probably a leafroller, but may also bore into plant stems. Host plants grapes and *Clematis*.

Plume Moths (Family Pterophoridae)

This family contains very small to minute moths with long legs; some are pests. They look like a "T" at rest. The wings are deeply notched, giving them a feathery, plumed appearance. These moths are often seen at lights. Larvae are leafrollers or borers, most covered with fine hairs.

B   *Emmelina monodactyla*

Upperside, Washington County

Wingspan up to ⅞ inch. Wings light gray with dark brown speckles. Habitat variable. Breeding resident with several broods. Flight year round. Common statewide.

Larva is very small, yellow-green with yellowish white dorsal stripe and gray hairs. Host plants morning glory, lamb's quarters, and Joe-pye weed.

A

B

Smoky Moths (Family Zygaenidae)

Small moths with narrow, mostly smoky gray or black wings.

A   Grapeleaf Skeletonizer Moth   *Harrisina americana*

Upperside, Washington County

Wingspan up to 1 inch. Black wings almost sheer, body black with a red-orange collar. Habitat variable, day fliers. Breeding resident with several broods. Flight April–October. Uncommon to common statewide.

Larva, aka Grapeleaf Skeletonizer, does exactly that in groups. Host plants grapes, Redbud, and Virginia creeper.

Hooktip and Thyatirid Moths (Family Drepanidae)

This is a very small family of moths. They overwinter in cocoons made with fallen leaves. The larva's head is usually horned or lobed. Larvae feed in loose shelters.

B   Rose Hooktip   *Oreta rosea*

Upperside, Logan County

Wingspan up to 1⅜ inches. The forewings have a hooked appearance. Wing color varies from all yellow to pinkish brown, or intermediate as in photo. Habitat forested areas. Breeding resident with two broods. Flight May–September. Local, uncommon statewide.

Larva is shades of gray and brown, mimicking a dead leaf, and has a knob on the thorax. Larva lacks anal prolegs and has a long "tail." Host plants viburnum and birch.

C   Dogwood Thyatirid   *Euthyatira pudens*

Upperside, Washington County

Wingspan up to 1⅝ inches. Forewings gray with distinctive pinkish white spots, hindwings grayish white. Both have checkered fringe and metallic sheen. Habitat forested areas. Breeding resident with one brood. Flight March–May. Local, uncommon statewide.

Larva is smoky dorsally, waxy grayish green laterally, with black spots on head. Host plant is Flowering Dogwood, primarily young foliage.

A

B

C

Sack-Bearers (Family Mimallonidae)

This family of medium-sized moths do not feed as adults. The forewings are hooked below the apex. Late-instar larvae build portable, open-ended "sacks" of silk and leaves. Larvae overwinter in these sacks, and pupate in spring.

A   **Scalloped Sack-Bearer**   *Lacosoma chiridata*
     Upperside, Sebastian County

Wingspan up to 1¼ inches. Forewings with hooked apex, wings scalloped. Sexually dimorphic: ♀ larger, forewings yellow to reddish brown, ♂ forewings dark brown. Slightly wavy brown lines and reniform spot on forewings in both sexes. Habitat woodlands and forested areas. Breeding resident with one brood. Flight April–September.

Larva thick in the middle (dark yellow), tapered at ends (mottled brown). Early instars spin a "net" on host plant leaf, and attach frass end-to-end on the outside. Later instars create the sack. Host plants members of the oak family.

True Silkworm and Apatelodine Moths (Family Bombycidae)

These medium-sized moths do not feed as adults. Apatelodine moths used to be in the family Apatelodidae. There are small transparent "windows" in the forewings. Larvae are very hairy. Pupae overwinter in the soil. True silkworms are native to Asia. The Chinese learned to unravel the silk from cocoons thousands of years ago, which is easier to do when the cocoons are boiled. Each cocoon is made from a single strand of silk, which may be 500 to 1,300 yards in length.

B   **Spotted Apatelodes**   *Apatelodes terretacta*
     Upperside, Franklin County

Wingspan up to 1⅝ inches. Aka Wild Cherry Moth. Forewings gray with brown lines and shading, brownish black patches near base, with "windows" near apex. Habitat fields, woodlands, and forested areas. Breeding resident with two broods. Flight May–August. Uncommon to common statewide.

Larva white with long silky hairs, looks "swept," with nine black hair clusters (hair pencils) along the body. The first and last of these pencils are longer than the others. Older larvae have black broken stripes on each segment and black chevrons. Prolegs are red. Host plants ash, maples, oaks, Black Cherry, and others.

A

B

What gained we, little moth? Thy ashes,
Thy one brief parting pang may show:
And withering thought for soul that dashes
From deep to deep, are best a death more slow.

—Thomas Carlyle
Tragedy of the Night Moth

Pyralid Moths (Family Pyralidae)

This is the third largest family of moths, small to medium size. The forewings are triangular and elongate; the hindwings are broader. Pyralids hold their wings in a position that makes them look like sticks, which is effective camouflage. The adults vary greatly in appearance. Larval habits are also variable: the main common characteristic is that they hide while feeding. They bore into plant tissue, roll leaves, make webs, are scavengers in leaf litter and even in beehives.

Some of the larvae are pests of food products, crops, and beehives. The European Corn Borer, Garden Webworm Moth, Celery Leaftier Moth, and Grape Leaffolder Moth are among them. The common names of the moths in this family usually describe what plant the larva eats and how it eats or conceals itself.

Since the family is so large, only four species could be treated in this book, and these were chosen to show characteristics of the family. Many can be observed at lights at night.

A   *Epigagis huronalis*
Upperside, Logan County

Wingspan up to 1 inch. Forewings narrow and translucent white with a hint of yellow in addition to yellow-brown lines and dark brown shading near apex. The hindwings have two distinct brown lines. Habitat forested areas. Breeding resident with several broods. Flight May–September. Uncommon to common statewide.

Larva life history and host plant needs work.

B   *Blepharomastix ranalis*
Upperside, Logan County

Wingspan up to ⅞ inch. Shiny wings yellowish tan with brown lines and spots. Spots in the middle of forewings hollow. Habitat variety of open areas including gardens, fields, waste areas, and woods. Breeding resident with several broods. Flight April–October. Uncommon to common statewide.

Larva life history needs work. Host plant lamb's quarters.

C   **Basswood Leafroller Moth**   *Pantographa limata*
Upperside, Logan County

Wingspan up to 1½ inches. Wings are white, shaded with yellow and brown. Spots in middle of forewing hollow. Hindwings have thin, slightly wavy brown lines. Habitat woodlands and forests. Breeding resident with two broods. Flight April–August. Uncommon to common statewide.

Larva is a leafroller on host plants basswood and oaks.

D   *Dolichomia olinalis*
Upperside, Logan County

Wingspan up to 1 inch. Wings rose to deep purple. Yellow am. and pm. lines on forewings, triangular at costa. Yellow fringe on all four wings. Moth rests with wings spread and abdomen curled upward. Habitat variable. Breeding resident with two broods. Flight May–September. Uncommon to common statewide.

Larva life history needs work. Host plant members of the oak family.

A

B

C

D

Life is a frail moth flying
Caught in the web of the years that pass.

—Sara Teasdale

Fruit and Leafroller Moths (Family Tortricidae)

This is a large family of fairly common moths, many of them considered pests. These small moths are mostly gray, brown, or tan in color with dark bands. A few are brightly colored. The best way to distinguish them from pyralids is to look at the square-tipped forewings. At rest, the wings are held rooflike over the body. The larvae are just as variable as the adults, with many being leafrollers, feeding in webs, or boring into plant material. Many overwinter as a larva in a cocoon.

Since the family is so large, only four species are treated in this book to show characteristics of the family. Many can be collected at lights at night.

Some of the pests in this family have interesting histories. The Codling Moth is an important pest of apples and other fruits, and is native to Europe. It dates back to 1819 in America. The Oriental Fruit Moth is another non-native species that is a pest of peaches. Larvae first bore into the twigs, then into the fruits. The Acorn Moth bores into acorns. The European Pine Shoot Moth attacks young pine shoots in the spring. There's probably a tortricid moth for every plant, many of them introduced species and widely distributed, at least as far as the range of their host plants.

A   Codling Moth   *Cydia pomonella*

Upperside, Washington County

Wingspan up to ⅞ inch. Forewings have gray-tipped brown scales with dark brown lines, creating a unique effect. Hindwings plain. Habitat orchards. Breeding resident with two broods. Flight April–November. Locally common in orchards statewide.

Larva bores into young apples. First generation pupates in the ground or under bark, second brood overwinters as a full-grown larva in a cocoon. Host plant primarily apple, but peach, quince, and walnuts are also used.

B   Filbertworm Moth   *Melissopus latiferreanus*

Upperside, Washington County

Wingspan up to ⅞ inch. Aka Acorn Moth. Wings rusty brown with bronze sheen and metallic bands across forewings. Hindwings brown with sheen. Habitat forests. Breeding resident with two broods. Flight May–October. Common in forests statewide.

Larva bores into acorns and wasps' oak-apple galls.

C   *Argyrotaenia alisellana*

Upperside, Washington County

Wingspan up to 1 inch. Forewings brown with cream-colored spots, hindwings white. Habitat open areas, woodlands, forests. Breeding resident with one brood. Flight May–June, perhaps longer. Local, uncommon to common statewide.

Larva life history needs work. Host plants members of the oak family.

D   Oblique-banded Leafroller   *Choristoneura rosaceana*

Upperside, Washington County

Wingspan up to 1⅜ inches. Forewing has a bronze color with brown shading and lines. Hindwing dirty yellow. Habitat variable, anywhere orchards and ornamentals grow. Breeding resident with at least two broods. Flight April–October. Common statewide.

Larva rolls leaves, makes a web, and is a pest. Host plants apple, holly, oaks, pines, and others.

A

B

C

D

Thus hath the candle singed the moth.

—William Shakespeare
The Merchant of Venice

Slug Caterpillar Moths (Family Limacodidae)

"Slug" caterpillar is such a harsh name for this family. For gardeners, the word "slug" conjures up images of the pests we desperately try to remove from our tender foliage. But in actual fact, looking at some slug caterpillars reminds me of snowflake designs and colorful Christmas tree ornaments. The larvae don't look much like the leps we are so used to. Short and fleshy, they even appear headless, but that head is just covered by part of the thorax. These caterpillars defend themselves as other leps do: they are either brightly colored to warn predators they are poisonous, or they mimic other poisonous animals.

Slug caterpillars move around a lot like snails; they glide rather than crawl, using suckers instead of legs. They develop in seven to nine instars. Mature larvae over-winter in a loose cocoon (prepupa) with an escape hatch at one end. Some have poisonous stinging spines and should not be handled. Some do not sting at all, and we have brave scientists to thank for that valuable information. As with bee stings, individuals react differently to the poisonous spines. Some people may be allergic or have an otherwise severe reaction to the stings of these caterpillars. When in doubt, *do not handle* any spiny caterpillar.

The small to medium-sized moths that these caterpillars become don't get a lot of attention. They have stout bodies and are hairy. Wings are rounded, mostly drab in appearance, but a few species have bright bands or patches. These moths are often seen at lights.

A   Skiff Moth   *Prolimacodes badia*
Upperside, Logan County

Wingspan up to 1⅜ inches. Forewings light brown with a bit of white at base; dark brown at upper edge (costa) forms a semicircular patch over most of the forewing, accented by white. Hindwings light brown. Habitat woodlands and forests. Breeding resident with two broods. Flight May–September. Common statewide, most common in the Interior Highlands.

Larva color is variable, but the shape is smooth and distinctive: flat on top with angled sides. Rear end of abdomen has a large round spot on last few segments, and a short, pointed "tail." Host plants a variety of trees and shrubs including blueberry, Black Cherry, maples, oaks, and willows.

B   Hag Moth (Monkey Slug)   *Phobetron pithecium*
Larva, Washington County

Wingspan up to 1⅛ inches. Sexually dimorphic; female larger with yellow and brown forewings, hindwings black, male wings translucent and resembling wasps. Day fliers. Some authorities suggest the female's legs mimic bees loaded with pollen. Habitat woodlands, forests, and fields. Breeding resident with two broods. Flight May–September. Rare to uncommon statewide, even in preferred habitat.

Larva, the Monkey Slug, reportedly mimics the cast skin of a tarantula. The larva can even lose arms and be all right. Although the spines reportedly do not sting some individuals, these larvae should be treated with caution. Host plants numerous, including apple, ash, chestnut, dogwoods, hickories, oaks, and Persimmon.

C   *Isa textula*
1) Upperside, Washington County
2) Larva, Washington County

Wingspan up to 1 inch. Wings brown with gray shading, hindwings brown. Habitat woodlands and forests. Breeding resident with two broods. Flight May–August. Locally common in forests statewide.

Larva, the Crowned Slug, is a wild sight. It is flattened, pale green, with lobes containing stinging spines radiating outward, somewhat like a crown. There are two dorsal red marks and additional stinging spines. Larva usually feeds on the underside of leaves. Host plants include oaks, basswood, beech, elms, hickories, maples, Black Cherry, and others.

A

B

C 1

C 2

Maidens, like moths, are ever caught by glare,
and Mammon wins his way when seraphs might despair.

—*Lord Byron*

Inchworm, Spanworm, and Looper Moths (Family Geometridae)

This is the second largest family of Lepidoptera. The moths are slender-bodied, ranging in size from small to medium, and are extremely variable. The wings are fairly broad and rounded. Some females are wingless. Antennae are noticeably more feathery-looking in males than in females. This family of moths also has a hearing organ, called the tympanum, on the abdomen. Many are observed at lights. The winter is passed differently by each species.

The larvae are typically long and slender. Some are missing the abdominal legs, and therefore move in the characteristic "looping" action. They typically feed on leaves and pupate in loose cocoons in leaf litter or in the soil. When disturbed, many of these caterpillars stand erect and motionless, resembling twigs for protection. This family contains a few pests that can defoliate trees.

A   Common Spring Moth   *Heliomata cycladata*

Upperside, Washington County

Wingspan up to ⅞ inch. Wings have black edges with metallic blue spots; most
of wings have cream coloring. Brown lines cross cream patch on forewings.
Habitat forest edges. Day flier but also found at lights. Breeding resident with
one brood. Flight April–June. Locally uncommon statewide.

Larva green, mottled with black, cream lateral stripe. Pupae overwinter on the
ground. Host plants Black Locust and Honey Locust. Both larva and moth are
easily overlooked.

B   Dimorphic Gray   *Tornus scolopacinarius*

Upperside, Logan County

Wingspan up to 1⅛ inches. Sexaully dimorphic; females have yellowish tan wings
with gray shading. Male wings brownish gray with wavy lines and mottled
appearance. Both sexes have a round black dot in the middle (discal dot) of the
forewings and checkered fringe on all wings. Habitat woodlands, forested areas.
Breeding resident with several broods. Flight February–November. Common
statewide in forests.

Larva life history needs work. Host plants are flowers, such as asters and coreopsis.

C   Tulip-Tree Beauty   *Epimecis hortaria*

Upperside, Logan County

Wingspan up to 2¼ inches. Wings broad, margins of hindwings scalloped. Salt-
and-pepper color with a zigzag pattern. Blends in perfectly with concrete.
Habitat woodlands and forests. Breeding resident with two broods. Flight
March–October. Common statewide.

Larva is stout, color variable with faint stripes and fine hairs. Pupa overwinters.
Host plants include Tulip-Tree, Sassafras, spicebush, and pawpaw.

A

B

C

A   Common Lytrosis   *Lytrosis unitaria*

Upperside, Logan County

Wingspan up to 2⅜ inches. Wings yellowish brown, heavily shaded and streaked, resembling tree bark. Female is larger and has grayer coloring. Habitat woodlands and forests. Breeding resident with one brood. Flight May–July. Uncommon to locally common statewide in forests.

Larva gray, looks very much like a twig. The first abdominal segment has a swollen area dorsally, and there is a pair of horns on the fifth abdominal segment. The first proleg has a black line that runs to the top of the body. The pupa overwinters. Host plants members of the rose family, especially hawthorn and Serviceberry, but also maples, oaks, and viburnum.

B   Forked Euchlaena   *Euchlaena deductaria*

Upperside, Washington County

Wingspan up to 1⅞ inches. Wings straw yellow with brown shading and black flecks. Black discal dots, more noticeable on hindwings. A brown line near the edge of the forewing continues down to the hindwing, where it forks, then straightens again. Habitat woodlands and forests. Breeding resident with two broods. Flight April–August. Common in Ozarks, uncommon elsewhere.

Larva life history needs work. Host plant Black Cherry.

C   Hübner's Pero   *Pero ancetaria*

Upperside, Washington County

Wingspan up to 1½ inches. Wing margins scalloped. Forewing dark brown from base of wing to pm. line, rest of wing light brown with two black spots on lower edge. Hindwings brown with black spots along lower wing margin. Habitat woodlands and forests. Breeding resident with two broods. Flight March–November. Uncommon statewide, but may be locally common in some regions.

Larva yellow to brown with wavy brown stripes and tiny hairs (setae). Pupa overwinters in leaf litter in a cocoon. Host plants alders, birch, and willows.

A

B

C

A   Oak Beauty   *Phaeoura quernaria*

Upperside, Washington County

Wingspan up to 2¼ inches. Wings slightly scalloped, olive brown with white patches along forewing costa and apex; brown shading, black lines, and black flecks give grainy appearance. Female larger than male. Habitat woodlands and forests. Breeding resident with one brood. Flight March–October. Uncommon to common in forested areas statewide.

Larva is gray or brown, the second thoracic segment raised. Thickened setae form fringe between prolegs. Pupa overwinters. Host plants a variety of trees including basswood, birch, elms, maples, oaks, and willows.

B   Kent's Geometer   *Selenia kentaria*

Upperside, Washington County

Wingspan up to 2⅛ inches. Wings unevenly scalloped, orange-yellow with white shading, mostly along forewing costa, with brown lines and flecks. Habitat woodlands and forests. Breeding resident with two broods. Flight March–August. Uncommon statewide.

Larva brown and thick, girth much thicker in the fourth and fifth abdominal segments, making this a great twig mimic. Pupa overwinters. Host plants many trees including basswood, beech, maples, oaks, Black Cherry, and willows.

C   Maple Spanworm   *Ennomos magnaria*

1) Upperside, Logan County
2) Larva, Logan County

Wingspan up to 2⅜ inches. Wings unevenly scalloped and look just like autumn leaves. Wings yellow-orange with brown shading and spotting, reddish brown near edges. Female larger than male. Habitat woodlands and forests. Breeding resident with one brood. Flight August–October. Common statewide.

Larva is variable in color from green to brown. It looks and feels like a twig. There is a large dark swelling on the second abdominal segment and there are bumps all over the body. The flat head sticks out in line with the rest of the body. The eggs overwinter. Host plants a variety of trees including ash, basswood, maples, hickories, holly, oaks, and willows.

A

B

C 1

C 2

A   Straight-lined Plagodis   *Plagodis phlogosaria*

Upperside, summer brood, Washington County

Wingspan up to 1⅜ inches. Summer brood is brown with straight black lines; hindwing has tan area at wing base. Spring brood is orange-yellow with purple shading. Habitat woodlands and forests. Breeding resident with two broods. Flight April–August. Locally common in forested regions, uncommon elsewhere.

Larva life history needs work. Host plants basswood, Black Cherry, and others.

B   Southern Pine Looper Moth   *Caripeta aretaria*

Upperside, Logan County

Wingspan up to 1½ inches. Forewing costa orangish brown, middle of forewing reddish brown. White, gray, and silvery accents on forewings and hindwings. Habitat pine barrens and forests. Breeding resident with one or two broods. Flight in April and in August. Rare to uncommon in pine and mixed forests statewide.

Larva life history needs work. Host plants members of the pine family. Pupa overwinters.

C   Wavy-lined Emerald   *Synchlora aerata*

1) Upperside, Logan County
2) Larva, Logan County

Wingspan up to 1 inch. Body and wings emerald green. Forewings and hindwings have wavy, toothed lines. Habitat open areas, such as forest edges and gardens. Adults often seen at porch lights at night. Breeding resident with several broods. Flight May–October. Common statewide.

Larva, aka Camouflaged Looper, is brown, black, and white. It has the interesting habit of disguising itself with plant parts. It is easiest to think of as described by David Wagner: a "Mardi Gras caterpillar that is out of costume only after a molt." The larva overwinters as a middle instar. Host plants various flowers, mainly composites. The larva pictured was disguising itself with blazing star bracts when I found it. I noticed the caterpillar movement as I was cutting back the stem, and grabbed Don to photograph it. He didn't see the caterpillar until I poked it, and he had to switch lenses because it was so small.

A

B

C 1

C 2

A   Common Tan Wave   *Pleuroprucha insulsaria*
Upperside, Logan County

Wingspan up to ⅞ inch. Wings tan to brown; brown lines and dots give moth a grainy appearance. Habitat open and variable, including grasslands, forest edges, and fields. Breeding resident with several broods. Flight May–October. Common statewide and easily overlooked.

Larva small and variable: may be yellow, green, gray, or brown, with shades of white and brown. Some features are only visible with a hand lens. The larvae feed side by side on flowers, so look for their waste (frass). The pupa overwinters. Host plants numerous, including asters, bedstraw, bittersweet, goldenrod, mimosa, oaks, ragweed, senna, sweet clover, and willows.

B   Sweetfern Geometer   *Cyclophora pendulinaria*
Upperside, Logan County

Wingspan up to ⅞ inch. Wings whitish gray with toothed black lines and specks, grainy appearance. There are two hollow discal spots on the wings: round on forewings, oval on hindwings. Habitat variable. Breeding resident with two broods. Flight April–September. Uncommon statewide.

Larva variable in color and pattern: may be green, brown, orange, or purplish brown; some individuals have a checkered pattern. Pupa overwinters exposed, much like a butterfly's chrysalis. Host plants alders, birch, blueberry, huckleberry, sweetfern, oaks, and others.

C   Chickweed Geometer   *Haematopis grataria*
Upperside, Washington County

Wingspan up to 1 inch. Yellow wings with pink lines and discal spot. Hindwing a shade brighter yellow than forewing; pink line crosses the discal spot. Habitat open areas, fields, vacant lots, weedy areas, forest edges, etc. Breeding resident with several broods. Flight spring to fall frost. Common statewide.

Larva mottled brown, may also be green. Cocoon overwinters. Host plants chickweeds, clovers, smartweed, and other low-growing plants.

A

B

C

A   Dark-banded Geometer   *Eulithis atricolorata*
Upperside, Washington County

Wingspan up to 1¼ inches. Forewing marbled with dark brown patches and narrow tan lines. Hindwing brown with white median line. Fringe checkered. Habitat woodlands and forests, perhaps open areas. Breeding resident with one brood. Flight May–July. Uncommon, known from the Ozarks.

Larva life history needs work. Host plant unrecorded.

B   Bent-Line Carpet   *Costaconvexa centrostigaria*
Upperside, Logan County

Wingspan up to 1 inch. Wings gray with grainy appearance due to many fine lines. There are tiny black discal dots on all the wings. Habitat variable, seen often in open areas such as forest edges. Breeding resident with two broods. Flight March–October. Uncommon to common statewide, easily overlooked.

Larva is brown with fine lines and hairs. Host plants knotweed, smartweed, and others.

A

B

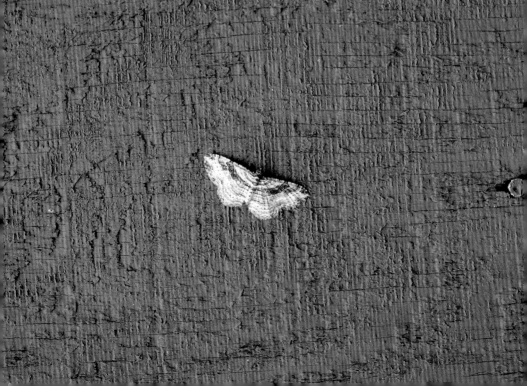

Bee to the blossom, moth to the flame;
Each to his passion, what's in a name?

—*Helen Hunt Jackson*

Tent Caterpillar and Lappet Moths (Family Lasiocampidae)

This is a small family of medium-sized moths, and all are very hairy. Adult moths do not feed, but they are usually seen at lights. The females are similar to males in color but are much larger. Larvae are colorful, have longitudinal stripes, and are very hairy. They usually feed at night and rest on bark during the day, where they are well camouflaged. Some, like the Eastern Tent Caterpillar, are forest pests. The moths pupate in a cocoon. Eggs are laid in masses and overwinter.

Eastern Tent Caterpillar nest

A   Large Tolype   *Tolype velleda*

Upperside, Washington County

Wingspan up to 2¼ inches. Body hairy, middle of thorax black. Abdomen gray to black. Wings gray with white veins and lines. Habitat woodlands and forests. Breeding resident with one brood. Flight September–October. Common in Interior Highlands, probably also in Coastal Plain.

Larva gray, with long silky hairs. The third thoracic segment has two red knobs followed by a black area not visible at rest. The larva is well camouflaged. The eggs overwinter in a mass covered with black scales from the female's abdomen. Host plants apple, ash, basswood, beech, Black Cherry, oaks, and others.

B   Dot-lined White   *Artace cibraria*

Upperside, Arkansas County

Wingspan up to 2½ inches. White body and wings with numerous black lines and dots on the forewings. Habitat fields, woodlands, and forest edges. Breeding resident with two broods. Flight June–October. Uncommon to common statewide.

Larva is flattened, mottled, and variable in color: may be charcoal black, gray, or brown. It looks as though it curls around twigs. Setae hide the head. Larvae feed at night and rest on bark during the day. The egg overwinters. Host plants oaks, Black Cherry, other members of the rose family, and probably additional trees.

C   Eastern Tent Caterpillar Moth   *Malacosoma americanum*

1) Upperside ♂, Washington County
2) Larva, Newton County

Wingspan up to 1¾ inches. Wings brown; forewing has white lines. Checkered fringe. Habitat fields, woodlands, and forest edges. Breeding resident with one brood. Flight May–June. Common statewide.

Larva, the infamous tent caterpillar, can be a serious pest. It is a pretty caterpillar, multi-colored with steel blue, black, orange, and white amidst all the long hair and white stripe on top (dorsal). The larvae live communally in a tent in the fork of a tree branch, and forage for food outside the nest. Larvae are often encountered on their way to make a cocoon in the springtime. Females lay egg masses that overwinter. Host plants include dozens of trees, especially apple, Black Cherry, and other members of the rose family.

A

B

C 1

C 2

As knowledge increases, wonder deepens.

—*Charles Morgan*

Giant Silkworm and Royal Moths (Family Saturniidae)

These are the largest, most familiar, and probably most beloved of our moths. The wingspan listed for each species is only a general guide, as some individuals may be much larger. Some of our silkmoths are small, so look at the antennae and stout bodies, usually very hairy. Male silkmoth antennae are feathery, or "plumose," and usually more elaborate than female antennae, which are threadlike in some species. This is because the male antennae are covered with thousands of microscopic sensors that detect pheromones (scent used to locate and attract mates). The females of each species release pheromones during a specific time, night or day, termed the "calling time." Some species can detect pheromones from several miles away. These moths live an average of ten to fourteen days and do not feed. The other life-cycle stages, however, can take a while.

Most people know the Luna Moth. It and some other large silkmoths have transparent eyespots encircled with color, presumably to startle predators. If you asked me where to start with moths, I would recommend this family. Many of the names come from characters in Greek mythology, like Io and Polyphemus.

The larvae are fleshy and extremely variable. They have hooks (crochets) on the bottom of the prolegs. Large mature larvae are so heavy their legs cannot support their weight, so they often hang upside down on the host plant to feed. The anal plate of the larva is armored or hardened, and the anal prolegs are also very strong. Some have stinging spines, some live together in groups, some are solitary, some have colorful tubercles or horns. As always, don't handle larvae with spines. Larvae feed mostly on trees and shrubs, and some are pests. The fecal pellets are large and distinctive with six grooves. The pupa stage varies: some of the giant silkworms spin a silk cocoon, either on the host plant or the ground, and others pupate in a chamber in the soil.

Attempts have been made to use the silken cocoons of the giant silkworms for an American silk industry, and have all failed. Silk garments and other textiles continue to be made from cocoons of the Asian silkmoth, a member of family Bombycidae.

Luna Moth antennae

A   Imperial Moth   *Eacles imperialis*

Upperside ♂ , Logan County

Wingspan up to 5½ inches. Females are larger and more yellow than males. This is the only giant silkmoth with yellow wings and shades of pinkish purple, orange or brown. Males have more pink shading than females. Habitat woodlands and forests. Breeding resident with two broods. Flight April–September. Often seen at lights, even after sunrise. Uncommon to common statewide, especially in the Interior Highlands.

Larva is variable in color: it may be green, brown, tan, red, etc., but has long setae and large white spiracles. It has spiny horns on the thorax. The larva pulls leaves of the host plant back over the body. The pupa overwinters in the soil. Host plants numerous, including basswood, Eastern Redcedar, elms, maples, oaks, pines, Sassafras, Sweet Gum, Sycamore, and walnuts.

B   Regal Moth   *Citheronia regalis*

1) Upperside, Logan County
2) Larva, Logan County

Wingspan up to 5 inches, aka the Royal Walnut Moth. At a close look, the forewing background color is gray, but the orange veins, shading, and yellow spots dominate. The hindwings are mostly orange with yellow at the base, unseen when moth is resting. Perfectly camouflaged against brick buildings. Habitat bottomlands, woodlands, and forests. Breeding resident with two broods. Flight June–September. Often seen at lights after sunrise. Uncommon to common statewide, mostly seen in the Interior Highlands.

Larva, the Hickory Horned Devil, is more famous, but is not seen as much as the adult. Perhaps the largest caterpillar in the country (and heavy!), it is a beautiful green with oblique white bands shaded with black. The orange and black thoracic horns give the larva its name, but they are harmless. The larva turns blue-green just before pupating. The pupa overwinters in the soil, sometimes through two winters. Host plants numerous, including ash, Black Cherry, cotton, hickories, lilac, pecan, Persimmon, sumacs, Sweet Gum, Sycamore, and walnuts.

Don and I used almost an entire roll of film on this caterpillar and had the best time doing it. Look at the photo of me holding this caterpillar on page 12 to get an idea of the size of the larva; it was five and a half inches long at the time. At press time, it was pupating in a jar. Rearing larvae isn't just for kids; it's also for kids at heart.

A

B 1

B 2

A Honey Locust Moth   *Sphingicampa bicolor*

Upperside, spring form, Washington County

Wingspan up to 2⅝ inches. Seasonally variable: forewings may be gray, yellow-orange, or brown with shades of rose and dark specks; there may or may not be tiny white reniform spots. Hindwings usually rosy. Habitat woodlands and forests. Breeding resident with several broods. Flight April–September. Uncommon to common statewide.

Larva green with tiny white dots all over body, with broad lateral white stripe and thin red stripe, and two pairs of thoracic horns. Larvae mature quickly, in three weeks in summer. The pupa overwinters in the soil. Host plants Honey Locust and Kentucky Coffee-Tree.

B Rosy Maple Moth   *Dryocampa rubicunda*

Upperside, Logan County

Wingspan up to 2 inches. A very small and pretty moth. Body and wings yellow to white. Pink legs and antennae. Forewings shaded with bright pink except median area. Hindwings have broad pink outer margin. Habitat bottomlands, woodlands, and forests. Often seen at lights and after sunrise; plays dead when handled. Breeding resident with several broods. Flight April–September. Common statewide.

Larva, the Green-striped Mapleworm, is green with frosty blue-green stripes and black thoracic horns. There is a rosy red patch under the spiracles near the rear end. Head orange-brown. These caterpillars can be pests in groups. The pupa overwinters in the soil. Host plants maples, oaks, and Box Elder.

C Pink-striped Oakworm Moth   *Anisota virginiensis*

Upperside, Chicot County

Wingspan up to 2¼ inches. Wings orangish brown with pink wing margins. Forewings are somewhat transparent in the middle, with a large white spot. Females are larger than males, and their wings are more rounded. Habitat woodlands and forests. Breeding resident with several broods. Flight May–October. Uncommon to common statewide.

Larva is pink and black striped, speckled with white dots, with a pair of black thoracic horns. Head yellow to orange-brown. Pupa overwinters in the soil. This larva can be a pest. Host plant red oak, but other oaks may be used.

A

B

C

A   Buck Moth   *Hemileuca maia*

Upperside ♂, Drew County

Wingspan up to 3 inches. This moth gets its name from deer hunting season, when it is most often seen. Wings are black with white bands in the middle, with a black-encircled reniform spot on forewings. The tip of the abdomen is red in ♂ black in ♀. Habitat barrens, woodlands, and forests. Day flier, most often seen in forests in early afternoon. Breeding resident with one brood. Flight October–November. Uncommon statewide; my theory is that it's overlooked.

Larva white to black in color, speckled with white dots and branched, poisonous spines. Be careful not to touch these as they pack a painful punch. The larvae feed together during the first few instars. Eggs are laid in clusters that overwinter. Larvae burrow into the ground to pupate, and pupae may pass through more than one season. Host plant scrub oak, but other oaks may be used.

B   Io Moth   *Automeris io*

1) Upperside ♀ and ♂, Logan County
2) Larvae, Logan County

Wingspan up to 3¼ inches. Sexually dimorphic with females larger, forewings reddish brown in ♀, yellow in ♂. Hindwings have a white-centered black and blue "bull's-eye" eyespot enhanced with black and rosy lines. Habitat fields, woodlands, forests, and riparian areas. Breeding resident with several broods. Flight May–September. Common statewide.

Larval first instars are dark brown, then orange, and turning green with red and white lateral stripes and branched spines as larva matures. Once again, don't touch the spines, the sting lasts for hours. The larva drops to the ground and rolls up when disturbed, much like a woolly bear. Pupa overwinters in a thin cocoon made of silk and leaf parts. Host plants numerous, including Black Cherry, blackberry, maples, hackberry, hibiscus, oaks, Sassafras, wisteria, and I have reared larvae successfully on *Lespedeza* (pictured).

A

B 1

B 2

Polyphemus Moth   *Antheraea polyphemus*

1) Upperside, Logan County
2) Underside with cocoon, Chicot County
3) Larva, Logan County

Wingspan up to 5 inches. One of the easiest moths to recognize, and probably the most common. Wings are light to reddish brown with pink-edged black and white lines. Wings have transparent oval spots encircled with black, blue, and yellow, creating large eyespots on the hindwings. Mainly nocturnal and seen at lights; found on tree trunks and buildings during the day. Habitat barrens, woodlands, and forests. Breeding resident with several broods. Flight April–September. Common statewide.

Larva is large, fleshy, smooth, and luminous green with vertical yellow stripes, body covered with silvery red or orange knobs with hairs (setae). Occasionally larvae make audible snapping sounds when eating. Larva pupates in a cocoon made with leaves and silk. Usually the cocoon stays on the ground, but occasionally the caterpillar attaches it with enough silk for it to remain on the host plant through the winter. Host plants numerous, including dogwood, elms, hickories, maples, oaks, willows, and members of the rose family such as apple.

1

2

3

A   Luna Moth   *Actias luna*

1) Upperside, Logan County
2) Larva, Logan County

Wingspan up to 5 inches. It's the only moth with long tails, which are often slightly curled. Wings are pale green with a few large transparent spots. A broad brown line leads to the spot in the forewing. Spring forms have pinkish purple wing margins, yellow in summer forms. Habitat open woodlands and forests, even seen at stadium lights during night games. Breeding resident with several broods. Flight March–September, through November in warm years. Common statewide.

Larva is fleshy, smooth, and lime green, with two thin yellow lateral stripes, red knobs (tubercles), and some setae. Larva spins a silk cocoon made with leaves, which overwinters on the ground in leaf litter. Host plants numerous including hickories, willows, maples, Persimmon, Sweet Gum, oaks, and walnuts.

The Luna is recognized by many people unfamiliar with leps. This moth often moves people emotionally with its beauty and grace.

B   Promethea Moth   *Callosamia promethea*

1) Underside ♀ and ♂, Washington County
2) Larva, Washington County

Wingspan up to 4 inches. Aka the Spicebush Silkmoth. Sexually dimorphic: ♀ bright reddish brown and larger, ♂ dark brown to black, forewing apex more angular, with whitish line and tan border, pink shading near apex. Males fly in late afternoon. Females seen at lights at night. Habitat field edges, woodlands, forests, and somewhat open areas. Breeding resident with at least two broods. Flight March–May, July–August. Uncommon statewide. This moth has declined in much of its range, perhaps partially due to a parasitic tachinid fly.

Larva pale green and smooth, with a bluish green cast. There are four bright red tubercles on the thorax, and a yellow one at the end of the abdomen, and lines of black dots over most of body. Head and legs yellow. Eggs are laid in clusters. Early instars are heavily banded and feed in groups, but as larvae mature they feed alone. The larva spins a cocoon in a curled leaf, attaching it to the host plant, where it overwinters. Host plants numerous, including Buttonbush, Black Cherry, lilac, magnolia, Sassafras, spicebush, Sweet Gum, and Tulip-Tree.

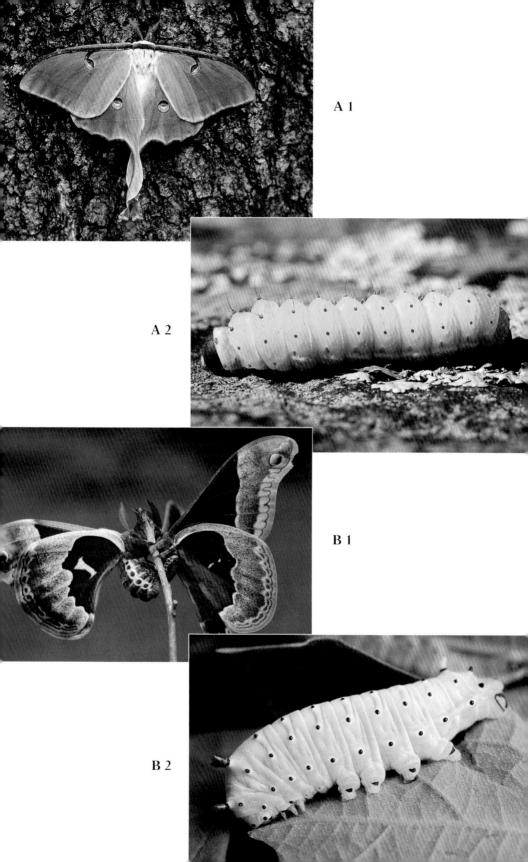

A 1

A 2

B 1

B 2

Cecropia Moth   *Hyalophora cecropia*

1) Upperside, Logan County
2) Larva, Logan County

Wingspan up to 6 inches. The name is pronounced see-CROW-pee-ah. The male is larger than the female, and is the largest moth in the United States. Body red with a white collar and abdominal bands. Wings are dark brown with red at base of forewings. Crescent eyespots on both forewings and hindwings are accented with red. White and red lines, distinctive wavy lines on the outer wing margins, and eyespots make this a spectacular moth. Habitat variable: found in cities, in the country, orchards, woodlands, and forests. Breeding resident with one brood, which emerge over a long period of time. Flight April–July. Uncommon to common statewide.

Larva frosty green with orange, yellow, and blue tubercles over the top and sides of the body. The dorsal tubercles on the thorax and first abdominal segment are globe-shaped and have minute black spines. The larva changes color as it grows, beginning as black, then orange, then frosty green. Legs are greenish yellow. This caterpillar may also be parasitized by tachinid wasps. Winter is passed in a large, distinctive silk cocoon. Somewhat banana- or spindle-shaped, it is attached lengthwise along a twig. Host plants numerous, including apple, Box Elder, Black Cherry, lilac, Sassafras, willows, elms, oaks, dogwoods, and maples.

1

2

What we see depends mainly on what we look for.

—*Sir John Lubbock*

Sphinx Moths (Family Sphingidae)

The sphinx moths are medium to large moths. Their bodies are stout, with the abdomen tapering at the end. They have big eyes. These are fascinating creatures; each species has more detail than is possible to print. The forewings are typically narrow, elongate, and pointed. The hindwings are smaller and rounded. The moths usually hold their wings rooflike at rest, so hindwings are seldom completely seen. The antennae are thickened in the middle, becoming narrower toward the tip. The proboscis in many species is long and strong, much longer than the length of the body, so these moths take advantage of many different kinds of flowers. Many are observed at lights, even after sunrise.

Some of the moths are pests, especially a few of the hawk moths, named for their swooping flight. Sphinx moths are strong fliers: some can fly at speeds up to thirty-five miles per hour.

The larvae are usually fleshy and smooth, with diagonal (oblique) lines and a dorsal horn on the rear end (caudal), or a button, giving rise to the name "hornworm." Much to the delight of gardeners, hornworms are often parasitized by braconid wasps. The wasp larvae eat the fat and vital organs of the larva and then pupate in white cocoons that resemble cotton swabs on the outside of the caterpillar, killing it. The larvae often elevate the head and thorax in a sphinxlike manner when disturbed, hence the common name. The winter is passed as a pupa, usually in a chamber in the ground or in a cocoon on the ground. The pupa looks like a pitcher, with the proboscis as the handle.

Blinded Sphinx (upperside)

A   Pink-spotted Hawk Moth   *Agrius cingulata*

Upperside, Logan County

Wingspan up to 4¼ inches. This is the only sphinx moth with pink bars on the abdomen. Forewings shades of gray and brown with long black dashes and two small white reniform spots encircled with black. Hindwing gray with black bands and pink shading. Habitat fields, woodlands, forests. Summer breeding resident with one or two broods. Flight June–October. Uncommon statewide, mostly seen in the fall. Numbers supplemented with migrants.

Larva is black with diagonal (oblique) pale pink stripes with dark pink dorsal lines on the thorax and black horn. Host plants sweet potato, morning glory, pawpaw, and Jimsonweed.

B   Rustic Sphinx   *Manduca rustica*

Upperside, Logan County

Wingspan up to 5 inches. Abdomen has three pairs of yellow spots. The forewing is light to dark brown with white, gray, and light brown mottling and black zigzag lines. Hindwings shaded with gray, black, and white. Habitat woodlands and forests. Strays north. Summer breeding resident with one or two broods. Flight July–October. Rare to uncommon statewide.

Larva green with seven black oblique lines edged below with yellow. Yellowish green horn is granulated. Host plants *Bignonia,* Fringe Tree, and jasmine.

C   Carolina Sphinx   *Manduca sexta*

1) Upperside, Logan County
2) Larva, Logan County

Wingspan up to 4½ inches. Forewing gray with black and white markings. There are six pairs of yellow spots on the abdomen. Hindwing with black zigzags that appear fused together. The forewing and hindwing fringe is spotted with white for a slightly checkered appearance. Habitat gardens, fields, and other disturbed areas. Breeding resident with several broods. Flight May–October. Common statewide.

Larva, the Tobacco Hornworm, is green with seven oblique lines and a pest. Horn is red, pink, or orange. Host plants tomato, tobacco, and other members of the nightshade family.

A

B

C 1

C 2

A   Five-spotted Hawk Moth   *Manduca quinquemaculata*
Upperside, Logan County

Wingspan up to 5½ inches. Wings are similar to the Carolina Sphinx, but the abdomen has five pairs of yellow spots. There is a prominent black line near the outer edge of the forewing shaded with grayish white. The hindwing black zigzag lines are sharper in this species than in the Carolina Sphinx. The forewing and hindwing fringe is gray. Habitat gardens, fields, and other disturbed areas. Breeding resident with several broods. Flight May–October. Common statewide.

Larva, the Tomato Hornworm, is very similar to the Tobacco Hornworm, but the horn is green and black, and the white lines form a "V" around the spiracles (chevrons). Larva can be green or blackish brown. Host plants tomato, tobacco, and other members of the nightshade family.

B   Catalpa Sphinx   *Ceratomia catalpae*
1) Upperside, Washington County
2) Larvae, Logan County

Wingspan up to 4 inches. Forewings dull light brown with black lines and dashes and indistinct grayish reniform spot encircled with black. Hindwings same color with darker brown lines. This sphinx moth does not feed as an adult. Habitat woodlands, forests, and urban areas. Breeding resident with several broods. Flight May–September. Uncommon to common statewide.

Larva, the Catalpa Worm, is seen more often than the adults, is a pest, and makes good fish bait. Larva varies in color, commonly black dorsally and yellow laterally, marked with vertical black lines and spots. Horn is long and black. The larvae feed in groups. Host plant catalpa; large numbers can defoliate a tree.

A

B 1

B 2

A   Pawpaw Sphinx   *Dolba hyloeus*
Upperside, Washington County

Wingspan up to 3 inches. Wings dark brown and dusted with white, with black
lines. Forewings have tiny grayish reniform spots circled with black, and black
zigzag lines in the middle. Hindwings dark brown with black zigzag lines and
white toward the lower wing margin. Habitat woodlands and forests. Breeding
resident with one brood. Flight June–September. Uncommon statewide.

Larva pale green with six distinct whitish oblique lines. Greenish white horn
darkens at tip. Host plants blueberry, holly, pawpaw, and sweetfern.

B   Laurel Sphinx   *Sphinx kalmiae*
Upperside, Logan County

Wingspan up to 4⅜ inches. Forewings brownish yellow; inner wing margin has
whitish line and black shading. Hindwings tan with a black basal patch, black
median line, and broad black outer wing margin. Habitat woodlands and forests.
Breeding resident with two broods. Flight May–August. Rare to uncommon
statewide.

Larva is green with orange spiracles and seven yellow oblique lines edged above
with black. There is a black band on the side of the head. The horn is blue with
black marks. Host plants laurels, ash, Fringe Tree, lilac, and privet.

C   Wild Cherry Sphinx   *Sphinx drupiferarum*
Upperside, Logan County

Wingspan up to 4½ inches. Forewings dark gray with whitish edging along costa
and outer wing margins. Barely visible reniform spot is edged with black.
Hindwings interchanging whitish and brownish black bands. Habitat woodlands
and forests. Breeding resident with one brood. Flight May–July. Rare to uncommon statewide.

Larva is green with white oblique lines edged above with purple. The horn is
reddish purple. Host plants apple, Black Cherry, peach, plum, lilac, and hackberry.

A

B

C

A   Blinded Sphinx   *Paonias excaecatus*

1) Upperside, Washington County
2) Larva, Logan County

Wingspan up to 3⅛ inches. Forewings rich dark brown and scalloped, with black dashes and dark brown reniform spot. Hindwings with a single blue eyespot encircled with black with pink shading. This moth does not feed as an adult. Habitat fields, woodlands, and forests. Breeding resident with several broods. Flight May–August. Common statewide.

Larva is variable: mainly green and granulose with oblique yellow stripes, red spots, front of head flattened and rimmed with a thin line, green horn, white spiracles encircled with black. Host plants numerous, including Black Cherry, apple, basswood, beech, elms, hawthorn, Hop Hornbeam, oaks, Serviceberry, and willows.

B   Small-eyed Sphinx   *Paonias myops*

1) Upperside, Logan County
2) Upperside, Logan County

Wingspan up to 2½ inches. Wings dark brown with a slightly purple sheen, forewings indented, lavender crescent at forewing apex, some additional lavender shading. Hindwings brown with blue eyespot surrounded by black and yellowish brown shading. Moth does not feed as adult. Habitat fields and woodlands. Breeding resident with several broods. Flight May–September. Common statewide, especially in the Interior Highlands.

Larva green, granulose, with a few large red spots, yellowish white oblique lines, and a green horn with small spines. Host plants Black Cherry, hawthorn, and Serviceberry.

A 1

A 2

B 1

B 2

A   Walnut Sphinx   *Amorpha juglandis*

Upperside, Logan County

Wingspan up to 3 inches. Wings scalloped, light brown with dark brown shading, with a pink or white tint, noticeable in bright light. The forewings have a small dark brown reniform spot. Adults do not feed. Habitat bottomlands, fields, woodlands, and forests. Breeding resident with several broods. Flight April–September. Common statewide in woodlands.

Larva is green with seven pairs of thin yellow oblique lines, the last line three times thicker than the others. Body covered with raised white granules. Reddish horn with white granules. Some individuals have reddish spots on the dorsal end of the oblique lines. Larva makes noise through spiracles if disturbed. Host plants hickories, Butternut, and walnuts.

B   Hummingbird Clearwing Moth   *Hemaris thysbe*

Upperside, Logan County

Wingspan up to 2¼ inches. Color varies. The wings have large unscaled areas, with the scaled areas brown and inner edge of outer forewing border uneven. The thorax usually olive green. Day flier seen hovering at flowers; mistaken for bees and hummingbirds. Habitat woodlands and forest edges, fields and gardens. Breeding resident with several broods. Flight April–September. Common statewide.

Larva green, granulose, with subdorsal yellow stripes, spiracles orange with white spots on top and bottom, curved bluish horn. Host plants viburnum, honeysuckles, and snowberry.

C   Snowberry Clearwing Moth   *Hemaris diffinis*

1) Underside, Logan County
2) Larva, Logan County

Wingspan up to 2 inches. Distinguished from the Hummingbird Clearwing by looking at the scaled areas of the wings, which can be a challenge when the moth is in flight. Most of the wing area is clear, the black scaled border smooth and thin. The thorax has black lines on the bottom (ventral) surface. Thorax and abdomen yellow with a broad black band. Habitat open areas, woodlands, and forest edges. Breeding resident with several broods. Flight April–September. Common statewide.

Larva blue-green above and yellow-green laterally, granulose. Spiracles are encircled with black, and each has a tiny white dot on the top and bottom. The horn is long, yellow at base, black from middle to tip. Host plants honeysuckles, snowberry, Dogbane, and Blue Star. Both clearwing moth species pupate in a cocoon on the ground.

A

B

C 1

C 2

A   Pandorus Sphinx *Eumorpha pandorus*

1) Upperside, Logan County
2) Larva, Logan County

Wingspan up to 4 inches. Forewings brown to olive green with brown to green patches and border along inner margin. Forewings have a double black reniform spot and pink streaks. Hindwings have two black patches and a short pink streak. Habitat fields, woodlands, forests. Breeding resident with several broods. Flight May–October. Common statewide in wooded areas.

Larva variable: green, orange, pink, or cinnamon with oval white or yellow spots surrounding the abdominal spiracles. Head and first two thoracic segments swollen. Early instars have a thin curly horn that is lost and replaced by a "button" in later instars. Host plants *Ampelopsis,* other grapes, and Virginia creeper.

B   Achemon Sphinx *Eumorpha achemon*

Upperside, Washington County

Wingspan up to 4 inches. Forewing brownish pink with a dark brown patch at the apex and square brown patch in the middle of the inner wing margin, small patch near outer edge. Hindwings pink with light brown border and a broken black line near the anal angle. Thorax has triangular dark brown patches that do not meet in the middle. Habitat fields, woodlands, forests. Breeding resident with one brood. Flight June–August. Uncommon statewide.

Larva similar in color to Pandorus Sphinx, but the white spots surrounding the spiracles are long and angular. Host plants *Ampelopsis* and other grapes.

A 1

A 2

B

A   Abbott's Sphinx   *Sphecodina abbottii*

Upperside, Logan County

Wingspan up to 2⅞ inches. Forewings are scalloped with dark brown and black barklike pattern. Hindwings have a broad yellow band. Habitat fields, woodlands, and forest edges. Adults attracted to bait, horse urine, and males may engage in mud-puddling. Breeding resident with one brood. Flight April–July. Uncommon statewide.

Larva is variable from the beginning: young larva is whitish or blue-green with a raised orange knob instead of a horn. Later instars may be two color forms: brown with a barklike pattern, or with ten light green saddles. The orange knob is replaced by a black eyelike button, which even has a white reflective spot similar to a vertebrate eye. Touching the eye causes the caterpillar to squeak, thrash, and bite. Host plants *Ampelopsis,* other grapes, and Virginia creeper.

B   Hydrangea Sphinx   *Darapsa versicolor*

Upperside, Washington County

Wingspan up to 3⅛ inches. Forewings olive green with curved lines and purple-pink and white patches. Hindwings orange, some green and white along lower edge (anal angle) and apex. Habitat riparian areas. Breeding resident with one to two broods. Flight April–September. Local, rare to uncommon statewide.

Larva is green or red; abdomen mottled with white and has oblique white lines. Spiracles encircled with red, each with a tiny white dot on the top and bottom. Orange horn has a black dorsal line. Host plants Buttonbush, Wild Hydrangea, and Water-Willow.

C   Azalea Sphinx   *Darapsa pholus*

Upperside, Logan County

Wingspan up to 3 inches. Forewings reddish brown with light purple shading and straight dark brown bands. Hindwings orangish brown. Habitat woodlands and forests. Breeding resident with two broods. Flight April–September. Uncommon to common statewide.

Larva is green and thick, the head and thorax swollen, abdomen mottled with white and has oblique white lines. Spiracles encircled with red, each with a tiny white dot on the top and bottom. Horn is bluish purple. Host plants azaleas, virburnum, blueberry, and others.

A

B

C

Tersa Sphinx   *Xylophanes tersa*

1) Upperside, Logan County
2) Larva, Logan County
3) Pupa, Logan County

Wingspan up to 3¼ inches. Long pointed abdomen is easy to spot. Forewings light brown with dark brown lines. Hindwings have jagged black markings at base of wing, yellowish white in the middle. Habitat fields, woodlands and forests. Moth visits flowers and is attracted to lights. Breeding resident with several broods. Flight June–October. Common statewide.

Larva has two color forms, mottled brown or green with yellow oblique lines, subdorsal stripes, and eyespots. Thoracic segments swollen. The horn is black. Host plants buttonplant, firebush, and others. I have reared both color forms successfully on pentas in my garden.

1

2

3

White-lined Sphinx   *Hyles lineata*

1) Upperside, Logan County
2) In flight, Logan County
3) Green larva, Logan County
4) Black larva, Logan County

Wingspan up to 3½ inches. Forewings brown with broad pale tan stripe extending from base to apex crossed with white streaks on veins, gray shading along outer margins. These markings are visible even when the moth is hovering at flowers. Hindwings black with pink median band and black outer margin. Habitat gardens, fields, waste places, roadsides, and forest edges. Breeding resident with several broods. Flight April–October. Common statewide.

Larva is variable: bright green, yellow, or black with variable spot patterns. Stout horn is yellow or orange with variable blackened areas. Head, thoracic shield, and anal plate are either orange or green, and dotted with tiny spots. Legs are orange. Host plants members of the rose and evening primrose families and a variety of other plants.

1

2

3

4

Prominents (Family Notodontidae)

The prominents are a small family of medium-sized moths that deserve a second look. Most do not feed as adults. They are often seen at lights, and hold their wings rooflike over their bodies at rest. Females usually look similar to males in pattern, but are much larger.

Larvae feed on a variety of trees. When disturbed, several species elevate the front and rear ends of the body and "freeze" in position, wave fierce-looking, tail-like anal prolegs, regurgitate fluids, or shoot acid from a neck gland. Winter is usually passed in the pupal stage.

A   Drexel's Datana   *Datana drexelii*

Upperside, Washington County

Wingspan up to 2¼ inches. Forewings reddish brown with yellow lines and brown orbicular spots (sometimes inconspicuous) within dark brown patches near base. Hindwings yellow with broad reddish brown outer margins. Habitat woodlands and forests. Breeding resident with two broods. Flight May–September. Uncommon to common statewide.

Larva is yellow with black stripes and long hairs. Host plants blueberry, Sassafras, and witch hazel.

B   Spotted Datana   *Datana perspicua*

Larva, Logan County

Wingspan up to 2¼ inches. Forewings straw yellow with brown shading and brown lines, with brown orbicular and reniform spots. Hindwings pale yellow. Habitat woodlands and forests. Breeding resident with two broods. Flight May–September. Uncommon to common statewide.

Larva is black with yellow stripes and long hairs. Host plants sumacs.

A

B

A   White-dotted Prominent   *Nadata gibbosa*

Upperside, Logan County

Wingspan up to 2⅜ inches. Forewing yellow to rusty orange, with light brown shading and distinct brown and whitish lines. A pair of white dots in reniform spot gives the common name. Hindwings yellow. Habitat barrens, woodlands, and forests. Breeding resident with several broods. Flight April–October. Common statewide.

Larva is variable: bright yellow-green to waxy blue-green, stout with a pale dorsal stripe and small white dots. When disturbed, larva coils like a snake and displays yellow mandibles with black tips. Host plants are a variety of trees including oaks, alder, Black Cherry, maples, Wild Plum, Serviceberry, and willows.

B   Angulose Prominent   *Peridea angulosa*

Upperside, Logan County

Wingspan up to 2¼ inches. Forewings mottled gray with black double lines accented with orange. Forewing pattern continues to top of grayish white hindwings. Habitat barrens, woodlands, and forests. Breeding resident with two broods. Flight May–October. Uncommon to common statewide.

Larva is green or reddish pink with a whitish dorsal stripe and white and reddish pink stripes along the spiracles extending to the mandibles. The larva coils up defensively like the White-dotted Prominent. Host plants members of the oak family.

C   Double-toothed Prominent   *Nerice bidentata*

Upperside, Washington County

Wingspan up to 1½ inches. Forewings have distinctive double-toothed black band that separates the brown lower half of the forewing from the light-to-dark-brown upper half. The toothed edge of the black band is accented with white. Hindwings brown. Habitat fields, woodlands, and forests. Breeding resident with two broods. Flight April–September. Uncommon to common statewide.

Larva is blue-green, dorsally toothed with white shading. Host plant members of the elm family. Aka the Elm Leaf Caterpillar, it is well camouflaged as it feeds on toothed elm leaves.

A

B

C

A   White Furcula   *Furcula borealis*
1) Upperside, Logan County
2) Larva, Logan County

Wingspan up to 1⅝ inches. Wings white, with forewing pattern of dotted black lines and dark gray shading. Hindwings have two small dots near base, and wing margins are lined with black dots. Habitat woodland edges and forests. Breeding resident with two broods. Flight April–September. Uncommon to common statewide.

Larva yellow-green with brown diamond-shaped saddle over abdomen, "humped" appearance, and tail-like anal prolegs. Host plant Black Cherry.

B   Mottled Prominent   *Macrurocampa marthesia*
Upperside, Logan County

Wingspan up to 2¼ inches. Forewings black-brown from base to antemedial (am.) line; rest of wing has white, gray, and grayish brown lines. Hindwings grayish white with gray veins. Habitat barrens, woodlands, and forests. Breeding resident with two broods. Flight April–September. Uncommon to common statewide.

Larva is pale green and mottled with broken maroon rings, cream to white and red dorsal stripe, and long tail-like anal prolegs. Body usually has some red blotches. Oblique cream lines run through abdominal spiracles, the last one bent and continuing as a subspiracular stripe. Host plants oaks, beech, chestnut, maples, and poplars.

C   Pink Prominent   *Hyparpax aurora*
Upperside, Arkansas County

Wingspan up to 1⅜ inches. Forewings pink, yellow in the middle except along costa. Variations exist in which the pink is mixed with the yellow, making a softer pattern. Hindwings also variable, mainly whitish yellow with pink wing margins. Habitat dry areas, barrens, woodlands, and forests. Breeding resident with two broods. Flight April–September. Rare to uncommon statewide.

Larva is blue-green with fine white dots, an emerald-green saddle surrounded by white, and a network of thin red lines. Head mottled. First two thoracic segments marked with a dorsal reddish brown triangle. First and eighth abdominal segments have a small pair of reddish orange horns. Anal prolegs are peglike. Host plants members of the oak family and reportedly viburnum.

A 1

A 2

B

C

Tiger and Lichen Moths (Family Arctiidae)

This family of pretty moths has broad wings, and most are brightly colored. They are relatively small, one or two inches in wingspan. Antennae somewhat feathery in males, threadlike in females. Bright orange and red colors in moths usually act as a warning to predators. Some species of these moths fly during the day as well as night and are often seen at lights or bait. The moths hold the wings rooflike over the body at rest, keeping the hindwings very often unseen.

Larvae are usually hairy; the famous "woolly bears" are included here. Some are distasteful and display warning colors, too. Many chemical studies have been conducted in this family; the larvae ingest specific chemicals for protection, and these are also a precursor in the synthesis of male sex pheromones. Host plants vary from lichens to trees. Cocoons are made mostly of larval hair (setae) instead of silk. A few are pests you are probably familiar with.

A   Bella Moth   *Utetheisa bella*

Upperside, Washington County

Wingspan up to 1¼ inches. Aka Calico Moth and Rattlebox Moth. Wings distinctive: yellow forewings with rows of white-ringed black spots; hindwings pink with an uneven black border. Pattern and forewing color may vary slightly. Habitat open woods, forest edges, and gardens. This day flier visits flowers but may also be seen at lights at night. Breeding resident with several broods. Flight July–November. Rare to uncommon statewide.

Larva yellow with black cross bands and orangish brown head, not as hairy as other tiger larvae. Host plants legumes such as rattlebox, *Lespedeza*, lupine, and *Crotalaria*.

B   Joyful Holomelina   *Holomelina laeta*

Upperside, Arkansas County

Wingspan up to 1 inch. Forewings black. Hindwings red with a broad black border. Thorax black, abdomen red. Habitat open woods, forests, and gardens. This day flier may be seen on flowers but also at lights at night. Breeding resident. Flight June–September. Uncommon statewide.

Larva life history needs work. Host plants dandelion and plantain.

A   Scarlet-winged Lichen Moth   *Hypoprepia miniata*

Upperside, Logan County

Wingspan up to 1½ inches. Wings and body red, gray shading on abdomen. Forewings have three broad gray lines; the middle one is short. Hindwings have a broad gray border. Pattern may vary in some individuals. Habitat woodlands and forests. Breeding resident with several broods. Flight June–August or September. Uncommon to common statewide.

Larva black mottled with yellow; also present are long shiny black spines. The larvae have anal combs that allow them to "flick" their fecal pellets a long distance. This seemingly bizarre behavior fools predatory and parasitic wasps that smell their way to their prey. Host plants lichens.

B   Black-and-yellow Lichen Moth   *Lycomorpha pholus*

Upperside, Logan County

Wingspan up to 1¼ inches. Wings and body bluish black. Base of the forewings and hindwings yellowish orange. Sometimes mistaken for a butterfly, beetle, or bee. Habitat open areas: gardens, fields, waste places, woodlands and forest edges. Moth is a day flier seen on flowers. Breeding resident with apparently one brood. Flight July–September. Uncommon statewide.

Larva life history needs work. Host plants lichens.

C   Giant Leopard Moth   *Hypercompe scribonia*

1) Upperside, Logan County
2) Larva, Logan County

Wingspan up to 3½ inches. Wings white; forewings with hollow blue-black spots in a "leopard" pattern, hindwings with black streaks on trailing edge and spots along outer margin near apex. Habitat woodlands and forests. Breeding resident with several broods. Flight April–September. Uncommon to common statewide.

Larva is a woolly bear, large and black with red bands on each segment. The black bristles are very stiff. Middle instars have orange patches. Like many woolly bears, the larvae are often seen in the fall and spring. The larvae overwinter under logs, bark, or anywhere there is shelter. Larvae hide by day and feed at night, and roll up to expose red bands when disturbed. Host plants Black Cherry, dandelion, maples, oaks, plantain, sunflowers, violets, willows, and a wide variety of other plants.

A

B

C 1

C 2

A   Reversed Haploa Moth   *Haploa reversa*

Upperside, Logan County

Wingspan up to 2¼ inches. Forewings yellowish white with broad brown lines. Forewing pattern may vary; some individuals may be completely white. Hindwings are white. Habitat open fields, woodlands, and forests, seen during the day and at lights at night. Breeding resident with one brood. Flight May–July. Common statewide.

Larva can be variable, mostly black with red dorsal and tan lateral stripe, not as many bristles as woolly bears. Larva overwinters. Host plants peach, apple, elms, willows, and a variety of other plants.

B   Parthenice Tiger Moth   *Grammia parthenice intermedia*

1) Upperside, Lincoln County
2) Larva, Logan County

Wingspan up to 2¼ inches. Intricate wing pattern. Forewings black with pale yellowish lines forming triangles. Hindwings orange with pink shading, edged with black triangular spots. Habitat open areas. Breeding resident. Flight May–October. Uncommon statewide.

Larva brownish black with setae arising from yellow-orange warts; it is difficult to separate from other members of the genus. Larva overwinters. Host plants dandelion, ironweed, thistles, and others.

A

B 1

B 2

A   Figured Tiger Moth   *Grammia figurata*
1) Upperside ♂, Washington County
2) Upperside ♀, Washington County

Wingspan up to 1⅝ inches. Wing pattern extremely variable in both sexes. Forewing black with variable cream-colored lines. Hindwings usually red with a black border with discal spot in ♂; hindwing may be red with black border, one red spot, or be completely black in ♀. Habitat open areas, seen at lights. Breeding resident with two broods. Flight April–September. Uncommon to locally common in the western Ozarks.

Larva is similar to other *Grammia*. Host plants alfalfa, plaintain, and other low-growing plants.

B   Anna Tiger Moth   *Grammia anna*
Upperside, Logan County

Wingspan up to 2 inches. Can easily be confused with other members of the genus. Forewing color and pattern very similar to Parthenice Tiger Moths. Hindwings are yellow with black border and spots. Females vary in forewing pattern, and hindwings may be completely black. Habitat open areas, woodlands, and forest edges. Breeding resident with one brood. Flight May–July. Uncommon to locally common in the Interior Highlands, but good habitat statewide.

Larva is black, similar to other *Grammia*. Host plants a wide variety of herbaceous plants including clover and plantain.

C   Isabella Tiger Moth   *Pyrrharctia isabella*
Upperside, Arkansas County

Wingspan up to 2⅜ inches. Moth not as well known as the larva. Wings orangish yellow. Forewings have brown lines and are pointed. There are some brown spots near apex. Hindwings are lighter in color, with black spots on the margins. Habitat variable open areas, woodlands, and forests. Breeding resident with two broods. Flight April–August. Common statewide.

Larva is the infamous orange-and-black bristly Woolly Bear. The orange band is wider in mature larvae because black is replaced with orange during each molt. Often encountered crossing roads in the fall, why is unknown. Larva overwinters. Host plants numerous, including dandelion, lettuce, clovers, elms, maples, and asters. **Contrary to folklore, it cannot predict winter weather.**

A 1

A 2

B

C

A   Banded Tussock Moth   *Halysidota tessellaris*

1) Upperside, Logan County
2) Larva, Logan County

Wingspan up to 2 inches. Body is orange-yellow with bluish collar. Wings are translucent pale yellow. Forewing has thin irregular black bands. Hindwings are plain. Habitat woodlands and forests. Often found at lights. Breeding resident with two broods. Flight May–October. Common statewide.

Larva variable, ranging from yellowish brown to grayish black, with a dark dorsal stripe, covered with yellow or gray hairs. There are black and white hair pencils at the front and rear. The head is large and black, and there are dorsal yellow-orange markings with black stripes just behind it. Larvae are often found in the open, suggesting they don't taste very good to predators. The pupa overwinters in a cocoon that includes lots of larval hair. Host plants a wide variety of trees and shrubs including ash, elms, blueberry, grapes, hackberry, hickories, oaks, walnuts, Tulip-Tree, and willows.

B   Fall Webworm Moth   *Hyphantria cunea*

1) Upperside, Washington County
2) Larval nest, Logan County

Wingspan up to 1½ inches. Larva better known than moth. Wings white with a few grayish brown spots or no marks at all. Habitat variable, including city parks, open fields, urban sites, woodlands, and forests. Often seen at lights. Breeding resident with several broods. Flight April–September. Common statewide.

Larva, known as the Fall Webworm, is a major pest. Larva is variable in color, pale yellow to dark gray with black spots and long hairs. Larvae live together in messy communal webs that may stretch over entire branches and trees. These nests are common sights late summer into fall, and seen more often than individual larvae. The pupa overwinters. Host plants include over 400 different trees, including apple, Black Cherry, elms, hickories, maples, walnuts, willows, and larvae even eat herbaceous plants. No doubt you have already encountered them!

A 1

A 2

B 1

B 2

A   Yellow-collared Scape Moth   *Cisseps fulvicollis*
Upperside, Logan County

Wingspan up to 1½ inches. Body bluish black with orange collar. Forewings black and slightly translucent. Hindwings seldom seen, but are clear except for black wing margins and veins. Habitat open fields, meadows, and gardens. A day flier that is often seen on flowers. Can be mistaken for the Grapeleaf Skeletonizer Moth. Breeding resident with several broods. Flight April–November (or until frost). Common statewide, most often seen during the fall months, and reportedly migratory.

Larva variable: yellow, brown, or black, with a reddish orange dorsal stripe and broad black stripes. Hairs (setae) are light in color and coverage. Head orangish brown. Larvae are nocturnal, found at ground level, and overwinter. Host plants grasses and sedges.

B   Virginian Tiger Moth   *Spilosoma virginica*
Underside, Washington County

Wingspan up to 2 inches. Similar to Fall Webworm Moth. Wings white with small black spots. The abdomen has yellow side stripes and black dots. The forelegs (first pair) are white with yellow and black. Moth may turn on its side when disturbed, as pictured. Habitat variable, including open fields, gardens, woodlands, and forests. Breeding resident with two broods. Flight April–October. Common statewide.

Larva, the Yellow Bear, starts as yellow, but as it grows becomes variable in color. It may be yellow, reddish, grayish white, or black, and is very hairy. The pupa overwinters. Host plants numerous including field crops, maples, sunflowers, walnuts, and willows.

A

B

*Everything in life is speaking
in spite of its apparent silence.*

—Hazrat Inayat Khan

Cutworms, Dagger Moths, Underwings, and Other Noctuids (Family Noctuidae)

This is the largest family of Lepidoptera, and is incredibly diverse. Adult colors range from striking to drab. Size ranges from small to large. Several serious economic pests are in this family. No doubt you have been encountering these moths for quite some time; you just may not have known it. Some are migratory and a few have strayed into the state the same way some butterflies have strayed. The giant Black Witch has strayed into Washington County a few times, far away from its tropical range.

Knowing whether the moth you are looking at is a noctuid is the first obstacle. Since size varies, it is not a good guideline. The body is stout and hairy. The proboscis is well developed; most of these moths drink nectar or visit sugar bait. Although most adults are nocturnal, several are active during the day. You can walk right by underwings resting on tree trunks during the day and not even know it, or go caving in the Ozarks and find them hiding inside. Antennae are usually threadlike. One neat feature of these moths is the hearing organ (tympanum) on the thorax, used to detect bat activity. Some bats specialize on noctuids; they are a good food source for many animals. Noctuids such as the Eight-spotted Forester, in contrast, display warning colors.

The larvae are just as variable, some of them notorious pests that keep the University of Arkansas Extension Service and Entomology Department busy, and give gardeners a headache. There are numerous species of cutworms, armyworms, budworms, and the like. The larvae of most species are generalists, foraging on a wide variety of plants, dead leaves, even fungi. Depending on the species, pupation occurs in the soil, food plants, decaying wood, or in cocoons.

The small sampling in this book is intended to reveal the diversity of these moths, their importance, their beauty, and to help identify some of the worst pests.

Girlfriend Underwing (upperside)

A   Green Cloverworm Moth *Hypena scabra*
Upperside, Crittenden County

Wingspan up to 1⅜ inches. Narrow forewings and broad hindwings make moth look like an arrowhead at rest. Wings are a dull, drab brown; forewing barklike pattern varies. Habitat variable: open areas, fields, woodlands, croplands. Breeding resident with several broods. Moth is also migratory. Flight year round; adults overwinter and fly on warm days. They are common sights in homes and in log piles in winter.

Larva is green with thin yellowish white lateral stripes. Host plants numerous including clovers, alfalfa, soybeans, strawberry, Black Cherry, and willows.

B   Locust Underwing *Euparthenos nubilis*
Upperside, Washington County

Wingspan up to 2¼ inches. Fairly easy to recognize; look for four wavy black bands on the orangish yellow hindwings. In contrast, the forewings are gray with dark gray and brown lines and shading, white patch at top. Not a true underwing moth: too many hindwing bands. Habitat disturbed areas, woodlands, and forests. Often seen at lights. Breeding resident with two broods. Flight April–September. Common statewide.

Larva is stout and smooth, with tan, brownish yellow, or brown wavy stripes with alternating darker stripes, mottled appearance. Host plant Black Locust, and it is possible Honey Locust is used.

C   False Underwing *Allotria elonympha*
Upperside, Washington County

Wingspan up to 1⅝ inches. Most easily recognized by yellow-orange hindwings with black border. Forewings gray, mottled with white, black, and brown; a small grayish white crescent is near the middle. Habitat wet (mesic) woodlands and forests. Breeding resident with two broods. Flight March–July. Uncommon; distribution is not well known beyond the Interior Highlands. This little moth is easily overlooked.

Larva is smooth, much like a looper in that it's well camouflaged on bark or twigs. Mottled gray, pink, or brown with a ventral brown spot. Host plants Black Gum, hickories, and walnuts.

A

B

C

A   Moon-lined Moth   *Spiloloma lunilinea*

Upperside, Washington County

Wingspan up to 2⅛ inches. Wings pale gray with brown shading and wavy lines near outer margins. Forewing has black spots along costa. Body has a brownish black collar. Often found at lights and bait. Habitat woodlands and forests. Breeding resident with two broods. Flight April–August. Common statewide.

Larva slender, mottled brown with yellow dorsal and lateral stripes, knobs, and setae. Host plant Honey Locust.

The underwings, genus Catocala (kah-TOCK-uh-lah), are named for their bright hindwings, a direct contrast to their barklike forewing patterns. The colorful hindwings are thought to startle predators if the forewing camouflage fails. Adults are attracted to lights and bait; otherwise one might never see them hiding in plain sight on tree trunks. They also hide in caves during the day. There is one brood per year, and all our species overwinter as eggs. Because so many of these moths inhabit Arkansas, only a few can be pictured in this book.

Underwing larvae are tapered at both ends, and have dark spots on the bottom, bumps, and warts. Their colors resemble the bark and twigs of the host plants. Finding them can be tricky, but the best time to look is when the trees are beginning to leaf out. The ventral side of mature larvae is often the same color as the adult wings. Larvae are strong and active, rest camouflaged in crevices or leaf litter by day, feed at night, and make a sparse cocoon in leaf litter. See References and Resources sections for articles and websites that feature the underwings.

B   The Betrothed   *Catocala innubens*

Upperside, Washington County

Wingspan up to 3 inches. Forewings mottled gray, white, and brown, with sharp wavy black lines. There is a white spot in the middle with a light brown bar through it. Hindwings black with orange bands and fringe. Habitat woodlands and forests. Flight June–September. Uncommon to common statewide.

Larva is light gray, somewhat mottled, with light tan near legs. Brownish saddle with black blotches across fifth and sixth abdominal segments. Host plant Honey Locust.

A **Glittering Underwing**   *Catocala innubens,* **form scintillans**
Upperside, Washington County

Wingspan up to 3 inches. This is a form, or variation, of The Betrothed. The forewings are mostly dark brown, outer wing margins shaded with grayish brown, brighter patch at the apex. Habitat woodlands and forests. Flight June–September. Uncommon to common statewide.

Larva is similar to The Betrothed. Host plant Honey Locust.

B **Dejected Underwing**   *Catocala dejecta*
Upperside, Washington County

Wingspan up to 3 inches. Forewings mottled gray with brown and bluish shading, sharp wavy black lines, dashes, and brownish gray reniform and subreniform spots. Hindwings black with white fringe. Habitat woodlands and forests. Flight June–October. Rare to uncommon statewide.

Larva is mottled gray. Host plants members of the hickory family.

C **Widow Underwing**   *Catocala vidua*
Upperside, Logan County

Wingspan up to 3½ inches. As the picture shows, forewings provide effective camouflage; wings pale gray with yellowish brown and black shading, heavy black lines, black dash parallel to wing margin, and yellowish brown reniform spots. Hindwings black with white fringe. Habitat woodlands and forests. Flight July–October. Common statewide.

Larva is gray with conspicuous fringe (setae) just above legs. Host plants pecan, Shagbark, Mockernut, and other hickories.

D **Clouded Underwing**   *Catocala nebulosa*
Upperside, Washington County

Wingspan up to 3⅝ inches. Forewings light reddish brown with a dark brown patch at base and light brown shading, wavy black lines; dark reddish brown apical patch at apex. Hindwings are dark orange-yellow with black bands and lighter orange-yellow fringe. Habitat moist woodlands and forests. Flight July through early fall. Recorded from the Ozarks.

Larva life history needs work. Host plant Bitternut Hickory.

A

B

C

D

A   Ilia Underwing   *Catocala ilia,* **form conspicua**

Upperside, Logan County

Wingspan up to 3⅛ inches. Forewings variable, mottled with dark gray and black, white in the middle. Reniform spot is solid white in this form. Hindwings have reddish orange bands; outer band scalloped near anal angle. Fringe pale orange, broad at apex. Habitat woodlands and forests. Flight June–September. Common statewide.

Larva resembles a twig with shades of pale gray, dark gray, and black. Host plants members of the oak family.

B   Joined Underwing   *Catocala junctura*

Upperside, Washington County

Wingspan up to 3⅛ inches. Forewings dark gray with black and brown lines and speckled with black. Hindwings light orange with black bands; median band does not reach wing margin. Fringe white with some orange. Habitat woodlands and forests; often hides in caves during the day. Flight June–October. Uncommon to common statewide.

Larva life history needs work. Host plants members of the willow family.

C   Scarlet Underwing   *Catocala coccinata*

Upperside, Washington County

Wingspan up to 2½ inches. Forewings mottled light gray and brown, with heavy black lines and black shading at base. Hindwings red (scarlet), fringe white with some red. Habitat woodlands and forests. Flight June–September. Local, uncommon to common statewide.

Larva is dark gray, mottled, with a few abdominal warty outgrowths; well camouflaged on twigs of same diameter. Host plant scrub oak.

A

B

C

A   Connubial Underwing   *Catocala connubialis*

Upperside, Washington County

Wingspan up to 1⅝ inches. Forewings white with sharp black zigzag lines, brown and gray bands along black-dotted wing margin. Hindwings yellowish orange with black bands; break in band along outer margin. Habitat woodlands and forests. Flight July–September. Rare to locally common statewide.

Larva is dark gray. Host plants members of the oak family.

B   Girlfriend Underwing   *Catocala amica*

Upperside, Logan County

Wingspan up to 1¼ inches. Forewings grayish white with brown band and black zigzag lines. Hindwings yellowish orange with broken black marginal band and no inner band. Habitat woodlands and forests. Flight June–September. Uncommon to common statewide.

Larva is pale gray to charcoal black with a somewhat mottled appearance. Dorsal hump on fifth abdominal segment, orange warts on eighth segment. Host plants members of the oak family, primarily white oaks.

C   Bilobed Looper Moth   *Megalographa biloba*

Upperside, Washington County

Wingspan up to 1⅛ inches. Forewings light brown with large silvery markings divided into two lobes. Hindwings grayish brown. Habitat variable: croplands, fields, gardens, other disturbed areas. Breeding resident with several broods. Seen during the day on flowers. Flight March–November. Migratory. Common statewide, sometimes emerging in large numbers.

Larva is frosty blue-green with lateral white lines and small spines; similar in shape to a looper. Green head has black bars on sides. Host plants garden crops, dandelion, and others. Larva may be a garden pest.

A

B

C

A   Pink-barred Lithacodia   *Pseudeustrotia carneola*

Upperside, Logan County

Wingspan up to 1 inch. Forewings dark brown with tan band and pinkish white bar from costa to reniform spot. Hindwings gray. Habitat moist woodlands and forests. Breeding resident with several broods. Flight May–September. Common statewide.

Larva life history needs work. Host plants goldenrod, smartweed, and docks.

B   Copper Underwing   *Amphipyra pyramidoides*

Upperside, Franklin County

Wingspan up to 2 inches. Forewing shiny brown with intricate pattern, pm. line and orbicular spot edged with white. Hindwing shiny copper color. Habitat woodlands and forests. Adults hide in tight places during the day. Breeding resident with one brood. Flight July–November. Common statewide.

Larva is blue-green with cream spots. White with yellow spiracular stripe extends from the thorax to anal plate, but missing from the third thoracic segment. The eighth abdominal segment has a humped appearance. The eggs overwinter. Host plants numerous trees and shrubs including apple, grapes, oaks, Redbud, rhododendron, and walnuts.

C   Goldenrod Stowaway   *Cirrhophanus triangulifer*

Upperside, Logan County

Wingspan up to 1¼ inches. Wings and body bright yellow, forewings streaked with orange, curved lines. Habitat fields, forest edges, power-line cuts, and other open areas. Moths camouflage themselves on yellow flowers during the day. Breeding resident with one brood. Flight August–September. Local, rare to uncommon statewide.

Larva life history needs work. Host plant Tickseed Sunflower.

A

B

C

A   Lobelia Dagger Moth   *Acronicta lobeliae*
Upperside, Logan County

Wingspan up to 2⅜ inches. Forewings gray with heavy black dashes. Hindwings grayish brown. Habitat woodlands and forests. Breeding resident with several broods. Flight April–August. Common statewide.

Larva is gray with cream stripes and lateral "skirt" of long setae. Body speckled with black spots, providing effective camouflage. Host plants members of the oak family.

B   Smeared Dagger Moth   *Acronicta oblinita*
1) Upperside, Washington County
2) Larva, Washington County

Wingspan up to 2⅛ inches. Forewings narrow and pointed, gray with dark broken lines, streaking, and spots; black-dotted wing margin. Hindwings are shiny white. Habitat open areas: barrens, wetlands, and reportedly orchards. Breeding resident with several broods. Flight March–September. Common statewide.

Larva is variable in color, usually a combination of black, yellow, red, and white, with a broad yellow spiracular stripe and reddish orange dorsal warts. Body covered with bands of setae. Larva makes a cocoon in leaves, unlike other dagger moths. Aka Smartweed Caterpillar. Host plants numerous including smartweed, willows, strawberry, cotton, elms, and apple.

C   The Green Marvel   *Agriopodes fallax*
Upperside, Logan County

Wingspan up to 1½ inches. Forewings pale green with large black triangular spots. There are a few round spots along the outer wing margin. Hindwings white with grayish brown marks. Habitat gardens, woodlands, and forests. Breeding resident with several broods. Flight April–September. Uncommon, known mainly from the Interior Highlands.

Larva is green with white lines and wrinkled black head. Host plant viburnum.

A

B 1

B 2

C

A   The Hebrew   *Polygrammate hebraeicum*
Upperside, Logan County

Wingspan up to 1½ inches. Forewings white with black spots and broken lines.
Hindwings white with grayish brown shading, darker at margin. Habitat swamps
and wet woodlands and forests. Breeding resident with several broods. Flight
April–September. Uncommon to common in the Interior Highlands.

Larva is bright green or blue-gray with sparse setae, cream stripes and yellow
spots. The pupa overwinters in a chamber the larva digs in bark. Host plant
Black Gum.

B   Beautiful Wood-Nymph   *Eudryas grata*
Upperside, Logan County

Wingspan up to 1⅞ inches. This moth looks like a bird dropping. Forewings
white with brown bands along costa and wing margins, thin gray streaks.
Hindwings yellow-orange with incomplete brown border. Habitat woodlands
and forests. Breeding resident with several broods. Flight April–September.
Uncommon to common statewide.

Larva is brightly colored with black, orange, and white rings and black spots,
humped at rear. Head and legs are orange with black dots. Larvae spend the day
exposed. In addition to having warning coloration, these and forester larvae bore
into wood or peat to pupate. Host plants *Ampelopsis*, other grapes, and Virginia
creeper.

C   Grapevine Epimenis   *Psychomorpha epimenis*
Upperside, Washington County

Wingspan up to 2⅛ inches. Body and wings black. Forewings have large white
patches and metallic gray shading. Hindwings have red patches. Habitat woodland and forest edges. A fast day flier seen at flowers and mud-puddling. Breeding
resident with one brood. Flight March–May. Uncommon to common statewide.

Larva is black and white. Orange head, shield, and rear hump have black dots.
The bright colors serve as a warning to predators. Larva creates a shelter in
young foliage by tying leaves with silk. Host plants grapes.

A

B

C

A Eight-spotted Forester   *Alypia octomaculata*

Upperside, Logan County

Wingspan up to 1⅜ inches. Wings black: four yellow spots and metallic blue bands on forewings, four white spots on hindwings. Body black except for yellow on part of the thorax and legs. Habitat woodland and forest edges. A day flier seen on flowers. Breeding resident with two broods. Flight April–June and August. Common statewide in spring, but not late summer.

Larva has black, white, and orange rings with black dots: warning colors. Sparsely covered with long white setae. Head, thorax, and rear hump orange with black dots. Host plants *Ampelopsis*, other grapes, and Virginia creeper.

B Armyworm Moth   *Mythimna unipuncta*

1) Upperside, Logan County
2) Larva, Washington County

Wingspan up to 1⅞ inches. Drab tan moth. Forewings with orange tint, speckled with black dots, one small white spot, and black line slanting inward from apex. Hindwings grayish brown with tan fringe. Habitat most open areas such as gardens and croplands. Seen at flowers, lights, and bait. Breeding resident with several broods. Flight year round. Common statewide, way too common, and migratory.

Larva, the Armyworm, is green or yellowish brown with stripes; larvae of large outbreaks darker. Larvae are notorious pests that feed in large groups at night, and devastate crop fields. Larva or pupa overwinters underground. Host plants numerous, including grains, garden plants, and ornamentals.

A

B 1

B 2

A   Variegated Cutworm Moth   *Peridroma saucia*

Upperside, Logan County

Wingspan up to 2 inches. Forewings brown to reddish brown with faint black lines. Faint brown reniform and orbicular spots. Dark patch slants inward from costa. Hindwing grayish white with brown margin. Habitat most open areas including forest edges. Breeding resident with several broods. Flight April–October. Common statewide.

Larva is a serious pest. This smooth cutworm is variable in color from gray to brown, has faintly colored stripes and an overall mottled appearance. Cutworms tunnel underground by day and feed at night, cutting foliage at the stem base and eating it elsewhere. Pupa overwinters. Host plants numerous, including grains, tomatoes, clovers, and also wildflowers.

B   Corn Earworm Moth (left)   *Helicopverpa zea*
    Tobacco Budworm Moth (right)   *Heliothis virescens*

1) Upperside, Washington County
2) Corn Earworm Moth larva, Washington County

Wingspan of Corn Earworm Moth up to 1⅞ inches. Forewings yellowish tan with reddish brown and gray shading and marks. Hindwings whitish gray, dark gray border. Habitat disturbed open areas, especially fields. Breeding resident with several broods. Flight May–December, migratory. Common statewide.

Larva, aka Cotton Bollworm, is a serious pest. Variable with many different colors including tan, yellow, orange, red, green, and dark brown to black with thin white stripes and sparse setae. Larvae feed mainly on flowers and seeds. Pupa overwinters. Host plants numerous, mainly corn (larva feeds on outer end beneath husk), cotton, soybeans, tomatoes, peppers, and beans.

Wingspan of Tobacco Budworm Moth up to 1½ inches. Forewings pale green with three parallel lines and dark green reniform spot. Hindwings white with gray margin. Habitat disturbed open areas. Breeding resident with several broods. Flight May–October, migratory. Common statewide.

Larva, aka Tobacco Budworm, is variable with many different colors including green, yellow, and red with tiny black spines, small black bumps with setae, broad yellowish white lateral stripes. Pupa overwinters. Larvae eat flower buds, flowers, fruits, and seeds. Host plants numerous, including tobacco (larval pest), Ageratum, cotton, geranium, soybeans, and members of the rose family.

A

B 1

B 2

Additional Moth Families to Watch For:

Tineidae (Clothes Moths): small moths; larvae are responsible for eating wool, but some eat plant materials.

Gelechiidae: small moths with narrow forewings. Hindwing tips pointed, lower margin concave, like a closed fist with one finger pointing. Some have heavy fringe.

Gracillariidae (Leaf Blotch Miner Moths): minute moths; larvae feed on the leaf epidermis, tunneling or "mining" through it. Mines are blotch- or serpentine-shaped. Larvae darken the mine with their frass.

Oecophoridae: small moths; some resemble bird droppings. Larvae are leafrollers or make webs of host plant, even animal carcasses.

Elachistidae: very small moths; larvae make blotch mines in grasses. Adults have long and narrow wings.

Blastobasidae: small, dull moths. Larvae are scavengers; some bore into nuts.

Coleophoridae (Casebearer Moths): very small, wings narrow. Larvae mine in leaves and seeds, later living in portable cases made from plant material and frass.

Momphidae: small white moths with long, narrow, pointed wings. Larvae often feed in flower buds, seeds, or are miners. One species was recently named in honor of an entomologist from Arkansas. Most of the species are in one genus, *Mompha.*

Agonoxenidae: very small moths with narrow, pointed wings. Larvae feed in webs under leaves and in bark, pupate in a double-layered cocoon.

Scythrididae: very small, dark, mostly day-flying moths with short wings. Larvae are leaf miners or skeletonizers.

Yponomeutidae (Ermine Moths):small to medium moths with narrow, blunt wings. The adults at rest are shaped like sticks. Larvae live together in webs spun around host plant leaves. Larvae can be pests.

Plutellidae (Diamondback Moths): small moths with narrow wings. A few are pests of cabbage, and this family includes the destructive Mimosa Webworm.

Heliodinidae: very small day-flying moths with narrow hindwings and broad fringe. Adults brightly colored and hold the hindlegs up at rest. Larvae are leaf miners or feed on leaf surface.

Choreutidae: small, dark day-flying moths with broad wings. Larvae feed mostly on plant surface; a few live in hollow stems.

Lymantriidae (Tussock Moths): small to medium moths that do not feed as adults. Wingless females in some species. Larvae have dense, colorful hair tufts with poisonous spines used in the cocoon; even the eggs are laid with these hairs. The Gypsy Moth, a pest of forests, belongs to this family, and luckily there are no current outbreaks.

Butterfly and Moth Gardening

One of the simplest ways to enjoy butterflies, aid in their conservation, and to simply feel good is to plant a butterfly garden. Type the key words "butterfly gardening" into an Internet search engine, and the results will be over 71 million websites. This staggering number reflects the passion unleashed for both butterflies and gardening during the past decade. Thousands of books, videos, and magazine articles have been written on the subject. One wonderful aspect of a butterfly garden is that additional wildlife will likely be attracted to it. Just remember to enjoy your garden and subsequent butterflies as often as you work in it!

Creating and maintaining a carefully planned garden is land management because all stages of butterflies and moths will benefit from the habitat provided. For those with only a deck or patio, never fear: a container garden filled with the right flowers will provide adequate adult resources. Butterfly gardens are only limited by imagination and resolve to make them happen.

Why do most butterflies visit flowers? They drink nectar that is contained inside a floral device called a nectary. Most flower nectar is about 20% sugar. Studies show that many butterflies prefer flowers with a thin, diluted nectar concentration that contains sugars of low molecular weight and nitrogen-rich amino acids. Nectar, animal droppings, carrion, tree sap, and rotten fruit all contain sugars and/or amino acids (the building blocks of proteins) and provide energy. Thin nectar prevents water loss from the butterfly's body and prevents the proboscis from clogging. Bees, in contrast, appear to prefer thicker nectar that contains high molecular weight sugars.

Butterflies and wildflowers have a symbiotic relationship known as mutualism. Butterflies get nectar out of the bargain, and the flower is pollinated. Pollination is the process by which pollen (male gametophyte) from the male stamen of the flower is transferred to the sticky stigma on top of the female pistil. This is the first step in fertilizing the egg, which will eventually produce a seed. Each time a butterfly sips nectar from a flower, it gets covered in pollen. The pollen transfers from the butterfly to the stigma of the next flower. It thus makes sense for the flower to "advertise" its nectar content and make itself look appealing to butterflies.

Butterfly flower preferences are literally in the eye of the beholder. Butterflies see in the ultraviolet spectrum of light. Many flowers have a colored center known as a nectar guide that reflects ultraviolet light and advertises that nectar is present. This nectar guide even fades as some flowers age, communicating to the butterfly not to bother. In addition to seeing in the ultraviolet spectrum, butterflies have color vision that is more acute than ours. Think of the flower's nectar guide as an airport runway, guiding the butterfly in for its reward. Butterfly preferences, however, are not based solely on color. Butterflies must also be able to cling to the flower with their claws.

Flowers with spikes, globular heads, and horizontal surfaces are best. This gives the gardener a multitude of choices! Butterfly physiology is also involved, as some larger butterflies need tall flowers, or flowers in small, tight clusters to accommodate a shorter proboscis.

Moreover, butterflies are active early morning to dusk in the summer months, so they need flowers that are blooming during these times. Of course, a good butterfly garden has a variety of flowers blooming spring through frost. Otherwise, why visit?

Before planting begins, consider the following:

1.   Survey the area to determine the amount of space available for your garden.
2.   How much sun does the area receive and is it relatively free from wind?
3.   Do you have, or could you obtain, 1–3 large rocks for basking?
4.   Can you provide shelter in the form of shrubs, small trees, building eaves, fences, and log piles?
5.   Survey the neighborhood or surrounding area for butterflies. Do they fly through without stopping? If they do stop, what plants do they use?

Several butterflies are associated with seasonal wildflower changes, especially if their flight period is short or they migrate in the fall. For example, when Wild Plum, Redbud, and Rose Verbena (A) bloom in spring, search for Pipevine and Zebra Swallowtails, Falcate Orangetips, Henry's Elfin, Juniper Hairstreak, and Spring Azure. In early summer, when Butterfly Milkweed (B) and Purple Coneflower (C) bloom, anticipate fritillaries, crescents, the Coral Hairstreak, and skippers. Summer into fall, when goldenrod (D) and asters are blooming, the Monarchs, Painted Ladies, and Cloudless Sulphurs are more common.

Floral layering creates a better visual field for butterflies. Tall flowers not only attract large swallowtails and Monarchs, but also serve as garden focal points or to soften fences. Medium flowers come next, then smaller ones in front. Butterflies are attracted to combinations of colors and surfaces, giving gardeners a chance to play and experiment year to year with perennials and annuals.

Gardeners who wish to combine native wildflowers with domestics have many choices, both annuals and perennials. Many annual domestics or "cultivated" flowers do very well in containers. Some cultivated flowers, such as butterfly bush (*Buddleia*), are purchased as small shrubs at the nursery. These plants may mature to over fifteen feet tall and several feet wide, so consider this when choosing the site in which to plant them.

Many day-flying moths sip nectar from flowers, but greater diversity of moths can be seen nectaring at night. Visibility is better when flowers are planted near an artificial light source. When a giant Five-spotted Hawk Moth visits flowers, the breeze from its hovering wings can be felt. The long proboscis of sphinx moths enables them to drink nectar from long floral tubes, even though they frequently visit smaller flowers.

A

B

C

D

Ever wonder why a butterfly lays eggs on the host plant you provided one year, but not the next? It could be a pH, protein, or mineral imbalance. Butterflies and moths scratch the leaf surface with their feet and "test" host plants. Tropical Milkweed, for example, is preferred by Monarchs over Butterfly Milkweed as a host plant. Scientists theorize it's a difference in each milkweed's protein content. Some caterpillars feed on the host plant's flowers because there is more protein in them.

You get as much out of a butterfly garden as you put into it. Read the care instructions on each flowerpot and seed packet for water, fertilizer, bloom time, and sun or shade requirements. Arkansans are no strangers to hot summers, periods of drought, or mild winters. Watering and other garden chores become more of a responsibility during these times.

Good months for planting flowers and trees are October, November, April, and May. Seeds are best planted in fall, winter, or early spring. Butterfly gardening is also big business, and Arkansas is abundant with nurseries and garden centers to help you get started and keep your garden thriving year to year. Refer to the Resources section for helpful state agencies.

"Top" Wildflowers for Butterflies

Rose Vervain, aka Rose Verbena

Blazing Star, *Liatris* (A)

Bee Balm (mint) (B)

Lemon Mint (C)

Lance-leaved Coreopsis

Ironweed

Goldenrod

Butterfly Milkweed

Mountain Mint

Hyssop (mint)

Tickseed Coreopsis

Purple Coneflower

Asters

The "Rest of the Best" Wildflowers

Dame's Rocket (D)

Phlox

Ox-Eye Daisy

Black-eyed Susan (A, page 265)

Cardinal Flower (B, page 265)

Queen Anne's Lace

Blue Star

Cosmos

Rocket Larkspur

Fire Pink

Wild Onion

Tall Vervain

Red Mexican Hat

Sunflower

Dogbane

A

B

C

D

Native Trees, Vines, and Shrubs

Buttonbush

Ninebark

Ohio Buckeye (C, facing page)

Jessamine

Domesticated Flowers

Butterfly Bush, *Buddleia* (D, facing page)

Allium

Lantana (A, page 267)

Tropical Milkweed (B, page 267)

Ageratum

Zinnias

Marigolds

Pentas (C, page 267)

Mexican Heather

Impatiens (D, page 267)

Flowers for Moths

Petunias

Zinnias

Butterfly Weed

Moonflower, *Datura*

Lantana

Wild Hyacinth

Enhance the Experience

Water: Butterflies need water, and they obtain most of it through their natural diet. It's common knowledge that several species of male butterflies may gather in a mud-puddle club. Butterflies are attracted to moving water, which can be supplied from a slow drip, a misting attachment for your bird feeder, or a sprinkler. Place a wet clay saucer on the ground, put a rock in the center of a bird bath so butterflies can visit safely, create a pile of moist sand on the ground or in a clay saucer, water a mound of manure, or create a "waterless pond" with a garbage bag and gravel, which is described in Mikula's *The Family Butterfly Book,* to collect morning dew. Make moist sand even more attractive by adding a few teaspoons of sea salt.

Fruit: Nectar doesn't do it for all butterflies. For example, satyrs, Mourning Cloaks, Question Marks, Red-spotted Purples, and Hackberry Emperors seldom drink nectar. They sip fruit juice and sap. Some swallowtails, fritillaries, and others are attracted to fruit juice. Set out fruit slices, especially watermelon, and make a few slits along the surface so the liquid pools into little wells. Place fruit on a saucer among the flowers about four feet off the ground on a wooden stand or rock for visibility. Just remember to bring the fruit in at night to prevent spoilage and possible messes from visiting raccoons and other animals.

A

B

C

D

Sugar, Sand, and Manure: Butterflies can be fed a diluted sugar water mix: 1–2 teaspoons of table sugar in one cup of boiling water. A higher ratio is too thick. Saturate acid-free tissue paper with this and set it in a clay saucer about four feet off the ground on a wooden stand or rock. Moist sand mixed with sea salt can be arranged the same way, or create a pile of moistened cow manure.

Host Plants and Pesticides: Of course, to keep butterflies and moths around your property year round, consider planting their host plants in at least a small area of your garden or yard. If you can tolerate voracious caterpillars chewing leaves and some flowers, you can revel in watching metamorphosis. Pest species may invade. However, using a pesticide will wipe out not only the pest, but every other butterfly or moth (and a few other beneficial insects) that you do want in your garden. If the problem is limited to only a few caterpillars, just pick them off the plants.

Winterizing: Depending on the species, butterflies and moths overwinter in one of the four stages of the life cycle. A few spend the winter as adults, but most spend it as a chrysalis. A wood pile of stacked logs will provide a safe shelter for these butterflies, and is a more reliable option than purchasing a wooden butterfly house. If you use wood logs in a fireplace, check them for stowaways before you use them!

Select Lep Pests and Their Hosts

PLANT	BUTTERFLY / MOTH CATERPILLAR
Ailanthus	Ailanthus Webworm
Peaches	Peach Tree Borer
Apples & other fruit	Codling Moth
Cabbage, Broccoli	Cabbage White
Hickories	Tent Caterpillar, Fall Webworm
Oaks	Gypsy Moth
Evergreens	Bagworm
Cotton	Pink Bollworm
Tomatoes	Tobacco and Tomato Hornworm
Catalpa	Catalpa Sphinx
Squash	Squash Vine Borer
Soybeans	Armyworm
Corn	Corn Earworm
Grapes	Grape Leaffolder
Most flowers	Cutworm
Wax in beehives	Greater Wax Moth

A

B

C

D

Sampling of Popular Garden Host Plants and Caterpillars

PLANT	BUTTERFLY / MOTH CATERPILLAR
Milkweed	Monarch, Milkweed Tiger Moth
Parsley, Dill, Fennel	Black Swallowtail
Pipe Vine	Pipevine Swallowtail
Pentas	Tersa Sphinx Moth
Lantana	Gray Hairstreak
Sennas, Lupine	Cloudless Sulphur, Sleepy Orange
Legumes	Orange and Clouded Sulphurs
Cannas	Brazilian Skipper
Sassafras, Spicebush	Spicebush Swallowtail
Wafer Ash	Giant Swallowtail
Honeysuckle	Hummingbird and Snowberry Clearwings
Grape	Grapevine Epimenis, Beautiful Wood-Nymph
Passion-Vine	Variegated and Gulf Fritillaries
Cherry	Tiger Swallowtail, Red-spotted Purple
Pawpaw	Zebra Swallowtail
Hickory	Hickory Horned Devil (Regal Moth), Maple Spanworm
Eastern Redcedar	Juniper Hairstreak
Big Bluestem	Dusky Roadside-Skipper
Black Locust	Silver-spotted Skipper, Funereal Duskywing, Locust Underwing
Willow	Viceroy

Recommended Nurseries

Holland Wildflower Farm (seeds)
P.O. Box 328, Elkins, AR 72727
www.hwildflower.com

Pine Ridge Gardens (native plants)
832 Sycamore Road, London, AR 72847
www.pineridgegardens.com

Arkansas Butterfly "Hot Spots"

Butterflies can be found in nearly every habitat in Arkansas. The trick is to get outside and look around. Butterflies are even seen in our largest cities, with or without gardens. Monarchs are often seen flying over downtown Little Rock and Fort Smith during migration. It's hard to know where to begin looking for butterflies since there are so many choices! Fields, weedy areas, line cuts, prairies, savannahs, forests, national wildlife refuges, and nearly every watercourse can be butterfly havens. These areas are wild, but there are also many public gardens in Arkansas that attract butterflies each year. Of course, your home garden could already be teeming with butterflies.

    The sites featured in this chapter are intended to give the beginner someplace to start, and for the more learned, perhaps a new place to visit. This is by no means the limit of hot spots in the state. Bring this field guide, perhaps one or two others, a highway map, a pair of binoculars if you have them, a notebook and pen, and a camera for an optimal experience. If you are headed to a state park, call ahead and see if any interpretive programs or events are scheduled during your date of visit. Remember that for each spot, weather and time of year can affect butterfly populations, so be flexible in your expectations. Locations are listed by the regions described on p. 25, and their numbers correspond to the Arkansas map at the end of this section. Happy hunting!

Ozark Mountains

1. Lost Valley, near Boxley, on the Buffalo National River corridor, in Newton County, on 280 acres. Trail is 2.3 miles round trip, with 200 feet of elevation gain to Eden Falls. Wildflowers, natural bridge, caves, waterfalls, bluff shelter below 200-foot cliff are highlights in addition to butterflies. The trailhead is located at end of a spur road off Highway 43 one mile south of Ponca. Details on Lost Valley and the Buffalo River are in the *Buffalo River Handbook,* by Kenneth L. Smith. Lost Valley's Clark Creek runs through this area, providing a moist beech and basswood forest. Harvesters, swallowtails, and hairstreaks are highlights of spring and summer. The Upper Buffalo Wilderness Area offers a multitude of trail, canoeing, and camping opportunities, as well as elk sightings. For more information visit www.nps.gov/buff/lv-trail/htm, or contact the superintendent's Harrison office at 870-741-5443.

2. Devil's Den State Park, near West Fork, in Washington County. This 2,500-acre state park is located deep in the Lee Creek Valley of the Ozarks and offers plenty of trails through oak-hickory forest. Devil's Den is known for its bats, birds, caves, trails, and WPA and CCC cabins, but it also a great place to search for swallowtails, fritillaries, and hairstreaks. Several new moth species (family Gelechiidae) have been

described to science as a result of sampling studies completed in this park. To reach Devil's Den State Park, travel 17 miles southwest of West Fork on Highway 170 or travel 7 miles west from Winslow on Highway 74. For more information on the park's treasures, visit www.arkansasstateparks.com, devilsden@arkansas.com, or call 479-761-3325.

3. Bear Hollow Natural Area, between Eureka Springs and Huntsville. This 397-acre natural area is managed by the Arkansas Natural Heritage Commission (ANHC), and borders the Madison County Wildlife Management Area in northern Madison County, just a few miles off Highway 23. The Ozark Natural Science Center, an environmental education center, is located in the heart of the natural area. Trails wind across Bear Hollow Creek upland to bluff shelters and lots of wildflowers in a mixed hardwood forest. A variety of butterflies can be observed May–September in a variety of habitats ranging from grassland to riparian. Swallowtails, the Great Spangled Fritillary, hairstreaks, and migrating Monarchs are common to the area. It's also a good area for birding. For more information, visit the ANHC website at www.naturalheritage.com and the ONSC website at www.onsc.uark.edu or call the ONSC office at 479-789-2754.

4. Gaston's White River Resort, near Lakeview. Arkansas's premier trout fishing resort has a lot to offer nature enthusiasts. Gaston's offers fishing, lodging, a conference center, a restaurant, and a gift shop. A trail system, gardens, and a wildflower meadow offer hikers opportunities for wildlife viewing. Wildflowers and butterflies seem to peak in May, June, and September, and sometimes August in a year with sufficient rainfall. Butterfly highlights include Northern Metalmarks, fritillaries, crescents, and swallowtails. Located in Baxter County, Gaston's Resort is adjacent to Bull Shoals/White River State Park, which is also worth a visit. Learn more about Gaston's White River Resort at www.gastons.com or call 870-431-5252.

Arkansas River Valley

5. Mount Magazine State Park, near Paris. At an elevation of 2,753 feet, this 2,200-acre park is on Arkansas's highest peak. This park is famous for its butterflies, largely due to the Mount Magazine Butterfly Festival, held annually the last weekend in June. Miles of trails wind through 11 different ecosystems where over 85 butterfly and 375 wildflower species have been recorded. The USDA Forest Service and the state park work together to manage the park's resources, which include several species of concern. Diana Fritillaries are locally common here May–July, and again in September. This is one of the few places in Arkansas where you can see male Dianas covering orange Butterfly Milkweed every .1 mile on the roadsides in June. Below is a short butterfly highlights list by season, and the full list is available online and in the visitor center:

April–May	June–August	September–October
Pipevine Swallowtail	Pipevine Swallowtail	Swallowtails
Zebra Swallowtail	Zebra Swallowtail	Female Diana
Tiger Swallowtail	Tiger Swallowtail	Southern Dogface
Spicebush Swallowtail	Spicebush Swallowtail	Cloudless Sulphur
Falcate Orangetip	Silver-spotted Skipper	Sleepy Orange
Orange Sulphur	Funereal Duskywing	American Lady
Question Mark	Cloudless Sulphur	Painted Lady
Juniper Hairstreak	Gray Hairstreak	Gulf Fritillary
Spring Azure	Great Spangled Fritillary	Viceroy
Male Diana (late May)	Coral Hairstreak	Monarch
Great Spangled Fritillary	Northern Pearly-Eye	Ocola Skipper
Mourning Cloak	Diana Fritillary	Leonard's Skipper

Mount Magazine State Park is located 19 miles south of Paris, or 10 miles north of Havana on Scenic Highway 309. For more information contact 479-963-8502 or visit the park website at www.mountmagazinestatepark.com.

Ouachita Mountains

6. Bell Slough Wildlife Management Area, near Mayflower. This area is one of over 100 that are managed by the Arkansas Game & Fish Commission. The Commission manages these areas to benefit wildlife and people. Bell Slough's 2,040 acres include wetland and forest habitats that are home to an abundance of wildlife, including over 80 species of butterflies. There is a butterfly checklist available at the trailhead. The trail is 2.25 miles long, and interpretive signs help you along the way as to what wildlife you may see. Hunting is allowed in season, so check dates with the Commission before your visit. Butterfly highlights short list: Diana, Northern Metalmark, Byssus Skipper, Pipevine Swallowtail, White-M Hairstreak, Gulf Fritillary, Goatweed Leafwing, Hackberry Emperor, Tawny Emperor, Southern Pearly-Eye, Gemmed Satyr, and Monarch. An annual North American Butterfly Association (NABA) Fourth of July butterfly count is held each June. For more information and directions to Bell Slough, contact the Arkansas Game & Fish Commission at 1-800-364-4263 or visit their website at www.agfc.state.ar.us.

7. Pine-Bluestem Project Demonstration Area, near Needmore. Managed by the USDA Forest Service, Poteau Ranger District. This project is an example of effective management practices. Visit the Poteau Ranger Station Visitor's Center in Waldron and learn about the pine-bluestem project, the endangered Red-cockaded Woodpecker, and other subjects. Pick up a brochure that accompanies the project and travel to Needmore on Highway 71, and the brochure directions will guide you to six different stops explaining the management of the forest for the survival of the

woodpecker. As a result of opening the forest for the woodpeckers more wildflowers have bloomed, and more butterflies, including Diana Fritillaries, inhabit the area. May and June are peak months to visit the project. For more information, contact the Poteau Ranger District office at 479-637-4174, or visit the Ouachita National Forest website at www.fs.fed.us/r8/ouachita.

8. Pinnacle Mountain State Park, near Little Rock. This 2,000-acre park offers several hiking trails to the summit of Pinnacle Mountain, a central Arkansas natural landmark just west of Little Rock over 1,000 feet tall. Habitat diversity ranges from upland peaks to bottomlands along the Big and Little Maumelle Rivers, which create suitable habitat for many different butterflies throughout the year. The park also boasts the Arkansas Arboretum, 71 acres of native plants highlighting the natural divisions of Arkansas. It offers a .6 mile trail. For more information on this park, visit www.arkansasstateparks.com, e-mail pinnaclemountain@arkansas.com, or call 501-868-5806.

While in Little Rock, visit Two Rivers Park and Wildwood Park. Two Rivers Park is over 100 acres, located south of Asher Street, north of Arch Street Pike, and east of Geyer Springs Road. It is managed by Little Rock Parks & Recreation. Contact 501-371-4770 for more information or visit the City of Little Rock website, www..littlerock.org. Click on City Departments, then click on Parks and Recreation. The park has walking paths and nature trails, and is a good spot to search for butterflies. Wildwood Park is a performing arts center in West Little Rock, located in a 105-acre botanical garden. Wildwood has several different gardens, each with a different theme, and provides habitat for many of our common butterflies. Wildwood is open weekdays from 8 am-5 pm, and on designated weekends. Docents give garden tours. For more information about Wildwood, visit www.wildwoodpark.org.

9. Queen Wilhelmina State Park, near Mena. Located atop Arkansas's second highest peak, Rich Mountain, this state park has excellent butterfly habitat. It is located along the 54-mile Talimena Scenic Drive. Rich in scenery, the park has several hiking trails and abundant butterflies. Interpreters conduct a NABA Fourth of July butterfly count with park visitors each year, and "Wings of Wonder," a special-event weekend devoted to butterfly programs Labor Day weekend. As in most areas in the Interior Highlands, spring, summer, and early fall are butterfly peak times. Highlights include swallowtails, Diana Fritillaries, Painted Ladies, and migrating Monarchs. To visit the park, travel 13 miles west of Mena on Highway 88, or contact the park at 479-394-2863, or visit the park's website at www.queenwilhelmina.com, and also the Talimena Scenic Drive website at www.talimenascenicdrive.com.

10. Lake Catherine State Park, near Hot Springs. This state park's trail system winds through mixed hardwood-pine forest. The self-directed Falls Branch Trail crosses

Little Canyon Creek in several places, passes by a scenic waterfall on Falls Creek, and is home to an abundance of butterflies. Spring is the best time to go if you are interested in seeing hundreds of our "common" butterflies at once. Henry's Elfin, every kind of duskywing, hairstreaks, and Falcate Orangetips seemingly cover the landscape. This is the "go-to" place for the Silvery Blue. Swallowtails cover jessamine vines. Summer brings wildflowers like Indian Pink and Royal Catchfly; butterflies include hairstreaks, crescents, satyrs, and the occasional Diana Fritillary. The Horseshoe Mountain Trail winds through a mixed hardwood forest, rock formations, and glades. Olympia Marbles can be sighted along this trail March–April. The state park is located at the end of Highway 171. Contact 501-844-4176 or visit www.arkansasstateparks.com for more information.

Coastal Plain

11. Rick Evans/Grandview Prairie Wildlife Management Area & Conservation Education Center, located 2 miles north of Columbus. This 4,885-acre multi-use area is managed by the Arkansas Game & Fish Commission. This prairie represents the largest contiguous tract of blackland prairie in public ownership in the country. The land consists of improved pasture, woodlands, wooded draws, bottomland habitats, and native grasslands comprised of blackland prairie communities. Blackland prairie is a special deep, dark mixture of soil and calcareous deposits. The prairie richness that supports so much plant and animal life is believed to originate from abundant invertebrate and fungal flora found in the soil. Hunting is allowed, so check regulations for seasons before your visit. Hiking, wildflower walks, and wildlife viewing are recreational activities besides hunting. Take care with your footsteps to leave minimal impact on the prairie. Butterfly highlights include Pipevine Swallowtail, Giant Swallowtail, Diana Fritillary, Viceroy, Monarch, Hoary Edge, Swarthy Skipper, Byssus Skipper, Zabulon Skipper, and Delaware Skipper. There is a NABA Fourth of July butterfly count held here each year. For more information about Grandview Prairie and the Conservation Education Center, contact the office at 1-877-777-5580 or visit www.agfc.state.ar.us.

12. Miller County Sandhills, near Texarkana. This 184-acre area is managed by The Nature Conservancy and includes property owned by the ANHC. The sandhills are named for deep deposits of ancient marine sand, one of the few remaining sites in the state. The sand creates an open forest and has several rare plants adapted to this habitat. Spring wildflowers peak in early June. The area consists of open woodlands with no marked trails, so be prepared for a little rough walking. Over 50 butterfly species have been recorded at the sandhills, most of them our common favorites, but it's the habitat that will catch your eye. For more information contact The Nature Conservancy's Arkansas office at 501-663-6699 or visit www.nature.org.

Delta

13. Big Lake National Wildlife Refuge, near Manila. Big Lake NWR was changed from a free-flowing river system to a lake/swamp ecosystem by the New Madrid earthquakes of 1811–12. Today it consists of wooded swamps and open water. The shallow lake has an average depth of three feet. The swamp areas are characterized by stands of Black Willow, Buttonbush, and towering Bald Cypress trees. Trees on higher ground include cottonwood, hackberry, Red Maple, Sycamore, and a variety of oaks. This makes it an oasis for butterflies adapted to swamps, and for migratory waterfowl, beaver, and white-tailed deer. Approximately 5,000 acres of the refuge has been aside as a National Natural Landmark. April and May are a good time to visit if the habitat is not flooded. Butterfly highlights during this time are Black Swallowtail, Eastern Tiger Swallowtail, Checkered White, Falcate Orangetip, Cloudless Sulphur, American Snout, Pearl Crescent, Eastern Comma, Red Admiral, Goatweed Leafwing, Monarch, Silver-spotted Skipper, Juvenal's Duskywing, the Bronze Copper and the Least Skipper. For more information contact the US Fish & Wildlife Service at 870-564-2429 or visit their website at www.fws.gov/biglake.

Crowley's Ridge

14. Forrest L. Wood Crowley's Ridge Nature Center, near Jonesboro. This nature center is located on the southern edge of Jonesboro between Highway 1 and South Culberhouse Road. The nature center tells the story of Crowley's Ridge both indoors and outdoors. It is one of four nature centers operated by the Arkansas Game & Fish Commission. A large butterfly garden greets visitors as they walk to the building entrance. Gulf Fritillaries, Least Skippers, and other butterflies flutter around native and domestic flowers, even in the intense heat of August. The Habitats Trail is .25 mile long and circles the pond behind the nature center. This is also an excellent place for bird-watching. Admission is free, and the center is open daily year round, though the butterflies are flying when weather and wildflowers allow. For more information, contact the nature center at www.crowleysridge.org or call 870-933-6787.

Glossary

Abdomen: The third (posterior) body part of an insect.

Am. line: The antemedial line, which separates the basal and median areas of some moth forewings as in the Moth Upperside Wing Patterns drawing on p. 139.

Anal angle: Point where the outer margin and inner margin of wings meet; some field manuals call it the tornus.

Anal plate: Dorsal shield on top of a caterpillar's last abdominal segment.

Anal proleg: Proleg on last abdominal segment of a caterpillar.

Antenna(e): Sensory structure(s) on the insect head mainly used to smell.

Anterior: Front; in front of.

Apex: The tip, mainly referring to the outer tip of a butterfly's forewing.

Band: Colored pattern that runs around a caterpillar's body (aka cross band), like the black, white, and yellow bands on Monarch caterpillars on p. 107, or row of colored spots on an adult's wing, as in the Variegated Fritillary on p. 109.

Base: The wing area closest to the thorax.

Bask: The behavior of exposing the wings to the sun to warm flight muscles.

Bilobed: Divided into two lobes.

Bisect: To divide into two equal parts.

Brood: A generation that completes the life cycle each year.

Calling time: The period of time during which pheromones are released by female silkmoths to attract males; it often lasts a few hours and varies with each species.

Caterpillar: The eating and growth stage of butterflies and moths, aka larva.

Caudal: The hind end or tail; as in the caudal horn of a hornworm.

Cell: The area of an adult's wings completely surrounded by veins, forewing cell being more costal, hindwing cell more central. Aka discal cell.

Cell-end bar (spot): A thin line (or spot) of color on the outer edge of the cell area of a wing.

Chevrons: The "V"-shaped marks on a caterpillar or wing.

Chrysalis: Pupa of a butterfly.

Claviform spot: Spot on the forewing beneath the orbicular spot on some moths.

Club: Enlarged tip or "knob" of a butterfly's antenna.

Cocoon: The silken bag that encloses the pupae of many moths and skippers. Some cocoons incorporate leaves, soil, or other materials.

Collar: The dorsal, furry first part of the thorax just behind the head of adults. Some caterpillars have a smooth, colored collar.

Colonist: A butterfly that establishes a temporary or even permanent population in a new area.

Costa: The leading upper, or forward, edge of an adult's wings, aka the costal margin.

Cremaster: Hooklike structure at the "tail" end of the pupa.

Crepuscular: Mostly active at dawn or dusk.

Crochets: Hooklike structures on the bottom of a caterpillar's prolegs.

Dash: A sharp, short, often black line on the forewings of some moths.

Diapause: A temporary state of inactivity, when body functions slow down in order to permit survival during unfavorable weather conditions.

Dimorphism: Different forms for the sexes (sexual dimorphism) or two forms for one sex.

Discal spot (discal dot): A spot toward the end of the cell of a wing, seen more often on the hindwings. This spot is called a discal dot if small.

Diurnal: Active during the day.

Dorsal: The top side or upper surface.

Eclosion: The act of emergence from the pupa.

Emigrant: A lep that leaves an area, usually on a long-distance flight.

Entomology: The study of insects.

Estivate: To spend hot, dry periods in an inactive state.

Exoskeleton: The hard, protective outer covering, or "skeleton," of an insect's body.

Extirpate: To eliminate a species from an area.

Forewings: The forward, or first, pair of wings.

Frass: For the adults, excrement in pellet form; for the kids, caterpillar poop.

Fringe: A fine border of hairlike scales along outer wing margins, extending beyond the wing itself.

Genitalia: The structures used in mating.

Habitat: The place where an insect lives, its home. A proper habitat has the right food, shelter, water, and space.

Hair pencil: A bundle or cluster of long setae on a caterpillar's body.

Head: The first (anterior) part of the body.

Hibernaculum: A winter nest a caterpillar makes of a rolled leaf and silk.

Hibernation: The process of overwintering in an inactive state for many animals.

Hilltopping: The act of males flying to the top of a hill and searching for females.

Hindwings: The hind, or second, pair of wings.

Immigrant: A butterfly that enters a habitat, mainly from a long-distance flight.

Inner margin: The trailing, or hind, edge of the wing.

Instar: A larval stage between molts.

Invertebrate: An animal that lacks a backbone and internal skeleton.

Labial palpi: Pair of modified, furry mouthparts that house the coiled proboscis.

Larva: Second stage of the Lepidoptera life cycle, aka a caterpillar.

Lateral: Along the side.

Leafroller: Moth larva that hides inside leaves that it rolls.

Macrolepidoptera: An artificial category containing most of the larger moths and all the butterflies.

Median area: An area at the middle of the wing, bounded by the am. and pm. lines as shown in the Moth Upperside Wing Patterns drawing on p. 139.

Median line: A transverse line extending through the median area of the forewing of some moths.

Mesic: Habitat with a moderate amount of moisture.

Microlepidoptera: An artificial category containing several families of mostly small to very tiny moths.

Migrant: An insect that makes regular two-way, long-distance flights. "Migrant" and "immigrant" seem to be used interchangeably in some field manuals.

Molt(ing): The process of a caterpillar shedding its exoskeleton, aka ecdysis.

Mud-Puddling: A behavior of some male butterflies and moths. They gather singly or in groups at wet areas to imbibe salts, and also perhaps for "safety in numbers."

Mutualism: A symbiotic relationship from which both organisms benefit. The example used in this book is butterflies or moths and wildflowers. Butterflies and moths benefit from the nectar the flowers produce, and the flowers benefit because they are pollinated and are able to produce seeds.

Nectar: The sugary liquid found in many flowers; the principal food source for adult Lepidoptera.

Nocturnal: Active at night.

Oblique: Diagonal, or at an angle, referring to stripes on a caterpillar's body.

Orbicular spot: A round or elliptical spot in the middle of a moth's forewing close to the costa, like the spot found on Drexel's Datana on p. 219.

Osmeterium: The fleshy, retractable, odor-producing gland behind the heads of swallowtail caterpillars.

Outer margin: The outer edge of the wing.

Oviposit: To deposit or lay eggs.

Palp: A modified, furry mouthpart that houses the proboscis on one side; see labial palpi.

Parasite: An animal that lives and feeds on another animal.

Patrolling: Mate-locating behavior in which males fly through habitat searching for females.

Perching: Mate-locating behavior in which males perch on objects located where a female might pass.

Pheromone: Chemical scent secreted and released by animals, used here to attract or identify potential mates.

Plumose: "Feathery" in appearance, like the plume of a bird.

Pollination: The process, or transfer, of pollen from the stamen (male) to the pistil (female) that is necessary in order for a flower to produce seeds.

Pm. line: The postmedial line, which separates the median area from the outer margin of adult moth forewings.

Proboscis: The coiled tube butterflies and moths use to drink fluids.

Prolegs: The first pair of the legs on an adult or the fleshy abdominal legs on a caterpillar.

Posterior: Hind or rear.

Pubescent: Covered with fine, short hairs.

Pupa: The third developmental stage of Lepidoptera, the stage in which the transformation from caterpillar to adult takes place.

Reniform spot: A spot, usually kidney-shaped, in the outer part of forewing close to the costa, like the spot found on the Ilia Underwing on p. 245.

Riparian: Term used to describe habitat along streams and rivers.

Scales: The powdery, flattened, modified shingles that cover the wings and bodies of Lepidoptera.

Sexually dimorphic: Males and females of the same species possessing different colors, markings, and sometimes sizes, as in the male and female Diana Fritillary on p. 111.

Seta: A hairlike outgrowth from the body.

Spine: A sharp, immovable outgrowth from the body.

Spiracle: A circular or oval breathing hole that opens and closes, located on the sides of caterpillars and adults.

Spiracular: Somewhere near the spiracles, usually adjacent to or passing through the spiracles.

Spot band: A fairly uniform line of colored spots on an adult's wing or caterpillar's body.

Stigma: In male *Hesperia* skippers, a cluster of specialized scales, containing the pheromones on the forewing. In female flowers, the sticky part of the pistil.

Subdorsal: Just below the dorsal area, but not quite reaching the middle.

Subreniform spot: Spot just below the reniform spot in most moths, like the spot found on the Dejected Underwing on p. 243.

Subventral: Area above thoracic legs and prolegs but below spiracles of a caterpillar.

Tarsal claw: Claw at the end of an insect's leg.

Teneral period: The period following eclosion, when the wings expand and harden.

Territoriality: Behavior in which the male occupies and defends a particular spot by investigating and chasing away trespassers.

Thoracic legs: The three pairs of legs located on the thorax of a caterpillar, also called "true legs."

Thorax: The second part of an insect's body.

Tubercle: A small rounded projection or extension on a caterpillar's body, also called a knob.

Tympanum: Hearing organ found in many moths.

Ultraviolet: The part of the spectrum of light not visible to the human eye but very important to insect vision.

Ventral: The lower surface of an insect's body or wings, the underside.

Wax glands: glands located just above the legs of many grass skippers.

References

Allen, R., and R. L. Brown. 1991. The biota of Magazine Mountain (II): a preliminary list of the macrolepidopteran fauna. *Proceedings of the Arkansas Academy of Science.* 46: 18–21.

Allen, T. J., J. P. Brock, and J. Glassberg. 2005. *Caterpillars in the Field and Garden: A Field Guide to the Butterfly Caterpillars of North America.* New York: Oxford University Press.

Borror, D. J., C. A. Triplehorn, and N. F. Johnson. 1989. *An Introduction to the Study of Insects.* 6ᵗʰ ed. Philadelphia: Saunders College Publishing.

Brewer, J., and D. Winter. 1986. *Butterflies and Moths: A Companion to Your Field Guide.* New York: Prentice Hall Press.

Brock, J. P., and K. Kaufman. 2003. *Butterflies of North America.* New York: Houghton Mifflin.

Brown, R. L., and R. T. Allen. 1974. Larval foodplants and parasites of some Lepidoptera in Southeast Arkansas. *J. Lepid. Soc.* 28: 168–70.

Brown, J. W., et al. 2004. *Catalog of the type specimens of Gelechioidea (Lepidoptera) in the collection of the National Museum of Natural History, Smithsonian Institution, Washington, D.C.* Zootaxa: 510. Auckland: Magnolia Press.

Carlton, C. E., and L. S. Nobles. 1996. Distribution of *Speyeria diana* (Lepidoptera: Nymphalidae) in the highlands of Arkansas, Missouri, and Oklahoma, with comments on conservation. *Ent. News* 107: 213–19.

Covell, C. V. 1984. *A Field Guide to the Moths of Eastern North America.* Boston: Houghton Mifflin.

Dole, J. M., W. B. Gerard, and J. M. Nelson. 2004. *Butterflies of Oklahoma, Kansas and North Texas.* Norman: University of Oklahoma Press.

Ferris, C. D., ed. 1989. Supplement to: *A Catalogue/Checklist of the Butterflies of America North of Mexico.* Memoir No. 3, The Lepidopterists' Society.

Foti, T., and G. Hanson. 1992. *Arkansas and the Land.* Fayetteville: University of Arkansas Press.

Gall, L. F., and D. C. Hawks. 2002. Systematics of moths in the genus *Catocala* (Noctuidae). III. The types of William H. Edwards, Augustus R. Grote, and Achille Guenée. *J. Lepid. Soc.* 56(4): 234–64.

Glassberg, J. 1999. *Butterflies through Binoculars: the East.* New York: Oxford University Press.

Heitzman, J. R, and J. E. Heitzman. 1987. *Butterflies and Moths of Missouri.* Jefferson City: Missouri Department of Conservation.

Hodges, R. W., et al. 1983. *Check List of the Lepidoptera of America North of Mexico.* London: Cambridge University Press.

Holland, W. J. 1931. *The Butterfly Book*. 2nd ed. Garden City: Doubleday & Company, Inc.

Howe, W. H. 1975. *The Butterflies of North America*. Garden City: Doubleday & Company, Inc.

Hunter, C. G. 1995. *Trees, Shrubs, & Vines of Arkansas*. 2nd ed. Little Rock: The Ozark Society Foundation.

———. 1995. *Wildflowers of Arkansas*. 4th ed. Little Rock: The Ozark Society Foundation.

Masters, J. H. 1967. Observations on Arkansas Rhopalocera and a list of species occurring in northeastern Arkansas. *J. Lepid. Soc.* 21(3): 206–9.

Miller, L. D., and F. M. Brown. 1981. *A Catalogue/Checklist of the Butterflies of America North of Mexico*. Memoir No. 2, The Lepdopterists' Society.

Miller, J. Y. 1992. *The Common Names of North American Butterflies*. Washington: Smithsonian Institution Press.

Mitchell, R. T., and H. S. Zim. 1962. *Butterflies and Moths*. New York: Golden Press.

Moore, D. M. 1994. *Trees of Arkansas*. Little Rock: Arkansas Forestry Commission.

Moran, M. D., and C. D. Baldridge. 2002. Distribution of the Diana Fritillary, *Speyeria diana* (Nymphalidae), in Arkansas, with notes on nectar plant and habitat preference. *J. Lepid. Soc.* 56 (3): 162–65.

Opler, P. A. 2000. *Lepidoptera of North America 1. Distribution of Silkmoths (Saturniidae) and Hawkmoths (Sphingidae) of Eastern North America*. Contribution of the C. P. Gillette Museum of Arthropod Diversity. Fort Collins: Colorado State University.

Opler, P. A., and G. O. Krizek. 1984. *Butterflies East of the Great Plains*. Baltimore: The Johns Hopkins University Press.

Opler, P. A., and V. Malikul. 1998. *A Field Guide to Eastern Butterflies*. New York: Houghton Mifflin.

Opler, P. A., and A. D. Warren. 2004. *Butterflies of North America. 2. Scientific Names List for Butterfly Species of North America, north of Mexico*. Contributions of the C. P. Gillette Museum of Arthropod Diversity. Fort Collins: Colorado State University.

Paulissen, L. J. 1977. A checklist of the sphinx moths of Arkansas. *Proceedings of the Arkansas Academy of Science*. 31: 117–18.

———. 1978. Checklist of butterflies and skippers of Arkansas. Arkansas Academy of Science, Arkansas Biota Survey Checklist.

———. 1978. Checklist of the Saturnoidea of Arkansas. Arkansas Academy of Science, Arkansas Biota Survey Checklist 16.

———. 1982. Checklist of the sphinx moths of Arkansas. Arkansas Academy of Science, Arkansas Biota Survey Checklist 35.

———. 1985. Checklist of the underwing moths (Noctuidae) of Arkansas. Arkansas Academy of Science, Arkansas Biota Survey Checklist 42.

Pavulaan, H. 2003. Searching for the elusive *Megathymus yuccae*. *News Lepid. Soc.* 45(2): 48–49.

Pyle, R. M. 1981. *The Audubon Society Field Guide to North American Butterflies*. New York: Alfred A. Knopf.

————. 2002. *The Butterflies of Cascadia*. Seattle: Seattle Audubon Society.

Ross, G. N. 1995. *Everything You Ever Wanted to Know About Butterflies*. Baton Rouge: Gary Noel Ross.

————. 1998. Definitive Destination: Mount Magazine State Park, Arkansas. *American Butterflies*. 6(2): 24–33.

————. 2002. Social Butterflies. *News Lepid. Soc.* 44(2): 55, 63.

————. 2003. What's for dinner? A new look at the role of phytochemicals in butterfly diets. *News Lepid. Soc.* 45(3): 83–89, 100.

————. 2005. A time to drink. *News Lepid. Soc.* 47(4): 107, 111.

Ross, G. N., and M. C. Henk. 2004. Notes on eggs and first instar larvae of three species of Speyeria (Nymphalidae). *News Lepid. Soc.* 46(2): 53–57, 62–63.

Rouse, E. P. 1965. The swallowtail butterflies of Arkansas (Lepidoptera, family Papilionidae). *Proceedings of the Arkansas Academy of Science*. 19: 37–39.

————. 1968. The satyrs and wood nymphs of Arkansas. *Proceedings of the Arkansas Academy of Science*. 22: 29–31.

————. 1969. The Pieridae of Arkansas. *Proceedings of the Arkansas Academy of Science*. 23: 94–104.

————. 1970. The butterflies of Arkansas: Family Nymphalidae. *Proceedings of the Arkansas Academy of Science*. 24: 76–79.

Sanger, R., and P. McLeod. 1988. Noctuidae and Pyralidae species composition and frequency in blacklight trap collections from snap bean fields in northwest Arkansas. *J. Kan. Ent. Soc.* 61(1): 1-8.

Scott, J. A. 1986. *The Butterflies of North America: A Natural History and Field Guide*. Stanford: Stanford University Press.

Scott, J. A., and D. M. Wright. 1993. *Celastrina nigra* and its synonym *C. ebenina* (Lepidoptera: Lycaenidae). *J. Res. Lepid*. 30(3–4): 257–60.

Selman, C. L., and H. E. Barton. 1971. The relative abundance, seasonal distribution and taxonomy of the Sphingidae of Northeast Arkansas. *Proceedings of the Arkansas Academy of Science*. 24: 56–68.

Spencer, L. A. 2004a. Hunting Zebras in the Ozark Mountains. *The Ozarks Mountaineer*. 52(3): 7.

————. 2004b. Devilish Royalty in the Ozarks. *The Ozarks Mountaineer*. 52(8): 10–11.

————. 2005a. Building a Better Butterfly Garden. *The Ozarks Moutaineer*. 53(4): 10–11.

————. 2005b. A Hummer of a Disguise. *The Ozarks Mountaineer*. 53(5): 18–19.

————. 2005c. *Butterfly Gardening in a Nutshell*. Little Rock: Arkansas State Parks.

————. 2006. *Arkansas Butterfly Checklist*. 3rd ed. Little Rock: Arkansas State Parks (in press).

————., and J. B. Whitfield. 1999. Revision of the Nearctic Species of *Rhysipolis* Förster (Hymenoptera: Braconidae). *Trans. Entom. Soc.* 125 (3): 295–324.

Stokes, D., L. Stokes, and E. Williams. 1991. *The Butterfly Book: An Easy Guide to Butterfly Gardening, Identification, and Behavior*. Boston: Little, Brown and Company.

————. 2001. *Beginner's Guide to Butterflies*. Boston: Little, Brown and Company.

Wagner, D. L. 2005. *Caterpillars of Eastern North America*. Princeton: Princeton University Press.

Wiley, E. O. 1981. *Phylogenetics: The Theory and Practice of Phylogenetic Systematics*. New York: John Wiley & Sons, Inc.

Williams, B. E. 2001. Recognition of western populations of *Speyeria idalia* (Nymphalidae) as a new subspecies. *J. Lepid. Soc.* 55(4): 144–49.

Wright, A. B. 1993. *Peterson First Guide to Caterpillars of North America*. Boston: Houghton Mifflin.

Resources

WEBSITES

BugGuide
www.bugguide.net. A volunteer site focused on identification of insects and spiders; easy to read, user-friendly; a good site for beginners.

Georgia Lepidoptera
www.daltonstate.edu; edited by James Adams, Dalton State College, Georgia. Photographs and good references for southern butterflies and moths.

Northern Prairie Wildlife Research Center (USGS)
www.npwc.usgs.gov/resource/distr/lepid/bflyusa.htm
This website lists butterflies and moths recorded in each state and county; uncontrollable variables dictate how fast a new state or county record reaches the map. New records must be thoroughly documented. Biological information is provided for each species, most of which have photographs.

Moth Photographers Group
www.origins.tv/MothPhotographersGroup/mainmenu.htm.
This digital guide to moth identification welcomes new photographs and is managed by the Mississippi Entomological Museum at Mississippi State University. There are several links to additional moth sites.

STATE AND NATIONAL AGENCIES

Arkansas Natural Heritage Commission (ANHC)
1500 Tower Bldg., 323 Center Street, Little Rock, AR 72201
501-324-9619, www.naturalheritage.com

Arkansas Game & Fish Commission
2 Natural Resources Drive, Little Rock, AR 72205
800-364-4263, www.agfc.com

Arkansas State Parks
One Capitol Mall, 4A-900
Little Rock, AR 72201
501-682-1191, www.ArkansasStateParks.com

Arkansas State Plant Board
1 Natural Resources Drive, Little Rock, AR 72205
501-225-1598, www.plantboard.org

The Nature Conservancy
National Office
4245 North Fairfax Drive, Suite 100
Arlington, VA 22203, www.nature.org

Arkansas Office
601 North University Avenue
Little Rock, AR 72205
501-663-6699

Arkansas Audubon Society
This chapter of the Audubon Society is composed of people interested in Arkansas
birds and other wildlife. In addition to Arkansas birding information, this website has
educational links and downloadable brochures.
www.arbirds.org

University of Arkansas Dept. of Entomology
www.uark.edu/depts/entmolo
This website provides an overview of the department's academics, research, Arkansas
agricultural experiment station, and the arthropod museum. The museum link features an overview of the arthropod collection, with additional information on
Arkansas arthropods.

University of Arkansas Cooperative Extension Service
2301 South University Avenue, Little Rock, AR 72204
501-671-2000, www.uaex.edu

USDA Forest Service
Ozark National Forest
605 W. Main, Russellville, AR 72801
479-964-7200, www.fs.fed.us/oonf/ozark

Ouachita National Forest
Box 1270, Federal Building
Hot Springs, AR 71092
501-321-5202, www.fs.fed.us/r8/ouachita

US Fish & Wildlife Service
National Office
1849 C Street
Washington, D. C. 20240
www.fws.gov

Arkansas Ecological Services Field Office
110 Amity Suite 300
Conway, AR 72032
501-513-4470, www.fws.gov/southeast

ARBFLY-L Discussion List
This is an e-mail discussion list (list-serve) composed of users interested in Arkansas
butterflies. Once you have subscribed, you will be able to send a butterfly-related
question, observation, or message to a single address and it will quickly and auto-

matically be delivered to all other subscribers to the list. Any replies to your message will also be delivered to all subscribers. It is free of charge.

This list is hosted by the University of Arkansas, with thanks to Kim Smith, List Owner, Department of Biological Sciences, University of Arkansas. Any questions may be directed to kgsmith@uark.edu.

You must be a subscriber to post to the ARBFLY-L list. To post messages, send your message to ARBFLY-L@listserv.uark.edu. Remember to include your name and location at the end of your message. Example message to subscribe: subscribe ARBFLY-L Jane Doe.

LEPIDOPTERA ORGANIZATIONS AND SUPPLY HOUSES

Lepidopterists' Society
c/o Los Angeles County Museum of Natural History
900 Exposition Boulevard, Los Angeles, CA 90007-40457
www.lepsoc.org

North American Butterfly Association (NABA)
4 Delaware Road, Morristown, NH 07960
973-285-0907, www.naba.org

Xerces Society
This is an international nonprofit organization dedicated to protecting biological diversity through invertebrate conservation. Subscribers receive *Wings,* their popular magazine. The website has links to important conservation issues.
4828 SE Hawthorne Blvd., Portland, OR 92715
503-232-6639, www.xerces.org

Monarch Watch
Based at the University of Kansas, this organization focuses on education and citizen science. The website contains an abundance of information on the biology and conservation of the Monarch. Thousands of Monarchs are tagged each year by volunteers and provide much-needed data on the migration. Monarch tagging kits are available from the Monarch Watch Shop at http://shop.monarchwatch.org or by calling 800-780-9986.

University of Kansas office:
1200 Sunnyside Avenue, Lawrence, KS 66045
www.monarchwatch.org

Young Entomologists's Society, Minibeast Merchandise Mall
Educational materials and insect novelties.
Online catalog: http://members.aol.com/YESsales/minimall.html

BioQuip
Entomological supplies and books; parent/teacher section.
2321 Gladwick Street, Rancho Dominguez, CA 90220
310-667-8800, www.bioquip.com

BOOK RECOMMENDATIONS FOR TEACHERS, PARENTS, INTERPRETERS, AND BUG LOVERS

Imes, R. 1997. *Incredible Bugs: The Ultimate Guide to the World of Insects.* New York: Barnes & Noble Books.

Mikula, R. 2000. *The Family Butterfly Book.* Pownal: Storey Books.

Pyle, R. M., and S. A. Hughes. 1993. *Butterflies. Peterson Field Guide Coloring Books.* Boston: Houghton Mifflin.

Rosenblatt, L. M. 1998. *Monarch Magic.* Charlotte: Williamson Publishing.

Turpin, F. T. 1997. *The Insect Appreciation Digest.* Lanham: The Entomological Foundation.

Winter, W. D. 2000. *Basic Techniques for Observing and Studying Moths and Butterflies.* Memoir No. 5, The Lepidopterists' Society.

Arkansas Butterfly Checklist

This checklist includes the names of all butterfly species recorded in the state, following Opler and Warren 2004. For convenience, the following letter codes apply: C=colonist, regular or infrequent, E=extirpated, S=stray. If no letter is given, the butterfly is a resident, a designation that includes summer breeding residents.

Hesperiidae: Skippers

- [ ] Silver-spotted Skipper
- [ ] Long-tailed Skipper
- [ ] Gold-banded Skipper
- [ ] Hoary Edge
- [ ] Southern Cloudywing
- [ ] Northern Cloudywing
- [ ] Confused Cloudywing
- [ ] Outis Skipper, S
- [ ] Hayhurst's Scallopwing
- [ ] Sickle-winged Skipper, S
- [ ] Dreamy Duskywing
- [ ] Sleepy Duskywing
- [ ] Juvenal's Duskywing
- [ ] Horace's Duskywing
- [ ] Mottled Duskywing
- [ ] Zarucco Duskywing, S
- [ ] Funereal Duskywing
- [ ] Wild Indigo Duskywing
- [ ] Common Checkered-Skipper
- [ ] Tropical Checkered-Skipper, S
- [ ] Desert Checkered-Skipper, S
- [ ] Northern White-Skipper, S
- [ ] Common Sootywing
- [ ] Swarthy Skipper
- [ ] Clouded Skipper
- [ ] Least Skipper
- [ ] Southern Skipperling
- [ ] Fiery Skipper
- [ ] Leonard's Skipper
- [ ] Cobweb Skipper
- [ ] Meske's Skipper
- [ ] Sachem
- [ ] Peck's Skipper, C
- [ ] Tawny-edged Skipper
- [ ] Crossline Skipper
- [ ] Whirlabout
- [ ] Southern Broken-Dash
- [ ] Northern Broken-Dash
- [ ] Little Glassywing
- [ ] Arogos Skipper
- [ ] Delaware Skipper
- [ ] Byssus Skipper
- [ ] Hobomok Skipper
- [ ] Zabulon Skipper
- [ ] Broad-winged Skipper
- [ ] Yehl Skipper
- [ ] Dion Skipper
- [ ] Duke's Skipper
- [ ] Dun Skipper
- [ ] Dusted Skipper
- [ ] Linda's Roadside-Skipper
- [ ] Pepper and Salt Skipper
- [ ] Lace-winged Roadside-Skipper
- [ ] Carolina Roadside-Skipper
- [ ] Nysa Roadside-Skipper
- [ ] Common Roadside-Skipper
- [ ] Bell's Roadside-Skipper
- [ ] Dusky Roadside-Skipper
- [ ] Eufala Skipper
- [ ] Brazilian Skipper, C
- [ ] Ocola Skipper
- [ ] Yucca Giant-Skipper

Papilionidae: Swallowtails

- [ ] Pipevine Swallowtail
- [ ] Polydamas Swallowtail, C

- [ ] Zebra Swallowtail
- [ ] Black Swallowtail
- [ ] Ozark Swallowtail
- [ ] Eastern Tiger Swallowtail
- [ ] Spicebush Swallowtail
- [ ] Palamedes Swallowtail, S
- [ ] Giant Swallowtail

Pieridae: Whites and Sulphurs
- [ ] Florida White, S
- [ ] Checkered White
- [ ] Cabbage White
- [ ] Great Southern White, S
- [ ] Olympia Marble
- [ ] Falcate Orangetip
- [ ] Clouded Sulphur
- [ ] Orange Sulphur
- [ ] Southern Dogface
- [ ] Cloudless Sulphur
- [ ] Large Orange Sulphur, S
- [ ] Orange-barred Sulphur, S
- [ ] Lyside Sulphur, S
- [ ] Barred Yellow, S
- [ ] Mexican Yellow, S
- [ ] Little Yellow
- [ ] Sleepy Orange
- [ ] Dainty Sulphur

Lycaenidae: Coppers, Hairstreaks, and Blues
- [ ] Harvester
- [ ] American Copper
- [ ] Bronze Copper
- [ ] Great Purple Hairstreak
- [ ] Juniper Hairstreak
- [ ] Frosted Elfin
- [ ] Henry's Elfin
- [ ] Eastern Pine Elfin
- [ ] Coral Hairstreak
- [ ] Edward's Hairstreak
- [ ] Banded Hairstreak
- [ ] Hickory Hairstreak
- [ ] King's Hairstreak

- [ ] Striped Hairstreak
- [ ] Oak Hairstreak
- [ ] Red-banded Hairstreak
- [ ] Gray Hairstreak
- [ ] White M Hairstreak
- [ ] Cassius Blue, S
- [ ] Marine Blue, S
- [ ] Western Pygmy-Blue, S
- [ ] Eastern Tailed-Blue
- [ ] Spring Azure
- [ ] Summer Azure
- [ ] Appalachian Azure, C
- [ ] Silvery Blue
- [ ] Reakirt's Blue

Riodinidae: Metalmarks
- [ ] Northern Metalmark
- [ ] Swamp Metalmark

Nymphalidae: Brushfoots
- [ ] American Snout
- [ ] Monarch
- [ ] Queen, S
- [ ] Gulf Fritillary
- [ ] Julia, S
- [ ] Zebra, S
- [ ] Variegated Fritillary
- [ ] Diana Fritillary
- [ ] Regal Fritillary, E
- [ ] Gorgone Checkerspot
- [ ] Silvery Checkerspot
- [ ] Phaon Crescent
- [ ] Pearl Crescent
- [ ] Texan Crescent, S
- [ ] Baltimore Checkerspot
- [ ] Common Buckeye
- [ ] Question Mark
- [ ] Eastern Comma
- [ ] Gray Comma
- [ ] Milbert's Tortoiseshell, S
- [ ] Mourning Cloak
- [ ] Red Admiral
- [ ] Painted Lady

- [ ] American Lady
- [ ] Red-spotted Purple
- [ ] Viceroy
- [ ] Common Mestra, S
- [ ] Goatweed Leafwing
- [ ] Hackberry Emperor
- [ ] Tawny Emperor
- [ ] Southern Pearly-Eye

- [ ] Northern Pearly-Eye
- [ ] Creole Pearly-Eye
- [ ] Appalachian Brown, S
- [ ] Gemmed Satyr
- [ ] Carolina Satyr
- [ ] Georgia Satyr
- [ ] Little Wood-Satyr
- [ ] Common Wood-Nymph

Arkansas Moth Checklist

This checklist includes the names of moth species covered in the Moth Descriptive Text.

Yucca Moths: Prodoxidae
- [ ] Yucca Moth

Bagworm Moths: Psychidae
- [ ] Bagworm Moth

Cosmopterigid Moths: Cosmopterigidae
- [ ] *Euclemensia bassetellata*

Tropical Ermine Moths: Attevidae
- [ ] Ailanthus Webworm Moth

Clear-winged or Wasp Moths: Sesiidae
- [ ] Squash Vine Borer
- [ ] Riley's Clearwing
- [ ] Peachtree Borer

Carpenterworm Moths: Cossidae
- [ ] Carpenterworm Moth

Flannel Moths: Megalopygidae
- [ ] Crinkled Flannel Moth

Window-winged Moths: Thyrididae
- [ ] Mournful Thyris

Plume Moths: Pterophoridae
- [ ] *Emmelina monodactyla*

Smoky Moths: Zygaenidae
- [ ] Grapeleaf Skeletonizer Moth

Hooktip and Thyatirid Moths: Drepanidae
- [ ] Rose Hooktip
- [ ] Dogwood Thyatirid

Sack-Bearers: Mimallonidae
- [ ] Scalloped Sack-Bearer

True Silkworm and Apatelodid Moths: Bombycidae
- [ ] Spotted Apatelodes

Pyralid Moths: Pyralidae
- [ ] *Epigagis huronalis*
- [ ] *Blepharomastix ranalis*
- [ ] Basswood Leafroller Moth
- [ ] *Dolichomia olinalis*

Tortricidae: Fruit and Leafroller Moths
- [ ] Codling Moth
- [ ] Filbertworm Moth
- [ ] *Agryrotaenia alisellana*
- [ ] Oblique-banded Leafroller

Slug Caterpillar Moths: Limacodidae
- [ ] Skiff Moth
- [ ] Hag Moth (Monkey Slug)
- [ ] *Isa textula*

Inchworm, Spanworm, and Looper Moths: Geometridae
- [ ] Common Spring Moth
- [ ] Dimorphic Gray
- [ ] Tulip-Tree Beauty
- [ ] Common Lytrosis
- [ ] Forked Euchlaena
- [ ] Hübner's Pero
- [ ] Oak Beauty
- [ ] Kent's Geometer
- [ ] Maple Spanworm
- [ ] Straight-lined Plagodis
- [ ] Southern Pine Looper Moth
- [ ] Wavy-lined Emerald
- [ ] Common Tan Wave
- [ ] Sweetfern Geometer
- [ ] Chickweed Geometer
- [ ] Dark-banded Geometer

☐ Bent-line Carpet

Tent Caterpillar and Lappet Moths: Lasiocampidae

☐ Large Tolype
☐ Dot-lined White
☐ Eastern Tent Caterpillar Moth

Giant Silkworm and Royal Moths: Saturniidae

☐ Imperial Moth
☐ Regal Moth
☐ Honey Locust Moth
☐ Rosy Maple Moth
☐ Pink-striped Oakworm Moth
☐ Buck Moth
☐ Io Moth
☐ Polyphemus Moth
☐ Luna Moth
☐ Promethea Moth
☐ Cecropia Moth

Sphinx Moths: Sphingidae

☐ Pink-spotted Hawk Moth
☐ Rustic Sphinx
☐ Carolina Sphinx
☐ Five-spotted Hawk Moth
☐ Catalpa Sphinx
☐ Pawpaw Sphinx
☐ Laurel Sphinx
☐ Wild Cherry Sphinx
☐ Blinded Sphinx
☐ Small-eyed Sphinx
☐ Walnut Sphinx
☐ Hummingbird Clearwing Moth
☐ Snowberry Clearwing Moth
☐ Pandorus Sphinx
☐ Achemon Sphinx
☐ Abbott's Sphinx
☐ Hydrangea Sphinx
☐ Azalea Sphinx
☐ Tersa Sphinx
☐ White-lined Sphinx

Prominents: Notodontidae

☐ Drexel's Datana

☐ Spotted Datana
☐ White-dotted Prominent
☐ Angulose Prominent
☐ Double-toothed Prominent
☐ White Furcula
☐ Mottled Prominent
☐ Pink Prominent

Tiger and Lichen Moths: Arctiidae

☐ Bella Moth
☐ Joyful Holomelina
☐ Scarlet-winged Lichen Moth
☐ Black-and-yellow Lichen Moth
☐ Giant Leopard Moth
☐ Reversed Haploa Moth
☐ Parthenice Tiger Moth
☐ Figured Tiger Moth
☐ Anna Tiger Moth
☐ Isabella Tiger Moth
☐ Banded Tussock Moth
☐ Fall Webworm Moth
☐ Yellow-collared Scape Moth
☐ Virginian Tiger Moth

Cutworms, Dagger Moths, Underwings, and Other Noctuids: Noctuidae

☐ Green Cloverworm Moth
☐ Locust Underwing
☐ False Underwing
☐ Moon-lined Moth
☐ The Betrothed
☐ Glittering Underwing
☐ Dejected Underwing
☐ Widow Underwing
☐ Clouded Undewing
☐ Ilia Underwing
☐ Joined Underwing
☐ Scarlet Underwing
☐ Connubial Underwing
☐ Girlfriend Underwing
☐ Bilobed Looper Moth
☐ Pink-barred Lithacodia

☐ Copper Underwing
☐ Goldenrod Stowaway
☐ Lobelia Dagger Moth
☐ Smeared Dagger Moth
☐ The Green Marvel
☐ The Hebrew
☐ Beautiful Wood-Nymph

☐ Grapevine Epimenis
☐ Eight-spotted Forester
☐ Armyworm Moth
☐ Variegated Cutworm Moth
☐ Corn Earworm Moth
☐ Tobacco Budworm Moth

Additional Moth Families to Watch For:

Tineidae
Gelechiidae
Gracillariidae
Oecophoridae
Elachistidae
Coleophoridae
Momphidae
Agonoxenidae
Scythrididae
Yponomeutidae
Plutellidae
Heliodinidae
Choreutidae
Lymantriidae

Photographers

Eighty percent of the photographs were taken by Don R. Simons, who has been working for Arkansas State Parks for 23 years and is currently serving as Park Interpreter at Mount Magazine State Park. His photographs have been published in magazines, books, state park publications, and websites. He uses a Canon AE-1 with a 50 mm lens and natural light. Mounted specimens were photographed against a gray Kodak card with natural light. Two butterflies, the Southern Dogface (underside) and Goatweed Leafwing, were chilled prior to photographing only because the butterflies were difficult to photograph naturally. This also presented a backlighting opportunity. Both butterflies flew away after the photos were taken.

Special thanks are due to the following photographers who supplied their work as indicated by page number, letter, and photograph number when applicable.

Steven Hunter, of Fort Smith: 99A2, 119-2, 195A2

Norman Lavers, of Jonesboro: 29, 31B, 33B, 33D, 35A, 39A, 41A, 41C, 43B-C, 45A-D, 47B-C, 49A-B, 51B-C, 53A-C, 55B, 57C2, 73, 75B, 83B, 85, 87B, 89A, 93B, 95A, 97B, 101A, 101C, 109A2, 115C, 121A2-B, 123B2, 127-2, 129B2, 131A2-B, 133B-C

Donald Steinkraus, of Fayetteville: 143B, 161A, 165B, 165C2, 183C1, 189A, 195B, 235B, 247C, 251B2, 255B2, 257B

Index to Butterfly and Moth Common Names

Page numbers in bold refer to butterfly and moth species descriptions in the descriptive text.

Index to Butterfly and Moth Scientific Names

Alphabetical by genus and family with species names included.

Index to Caterpillar Host Plants

In addition to host plants, this index also includes non-plant food that caterpillars eat as indicated in the descriptive text. For further assistance in recognizing host plants, these botanical texts are recommended: Carl Hunter's *Wildflowers of Arkansas* and *Trees, Shrubs, & Vines of Arkansas,* and Dwight Moore's *Trees of Arkansas.* University libraries usually have texts on grasses and herbaceous weeds.